The
Answer Book

The Answer Book

by
Dr. Samuel C. Gipp, Th.D.

DayStar Publishing

P. O. Box 464 · Miamitown, Ohio, 45041

OTHER BOOKS BY
THE SAME AUTHOR

Job

A Practical and Theological Study of The Book of Acts

A Practical and Theological Study of the Gospel of John

An Understandable History of The Bible

Living With Pain

Answers To the Ravings of a Mad Plunger

Reading and Understanding the Variations
Between the Critical Apparatuses of
Nestle's 25th and 26th Editions of
the *Novum Testamentum-Graece*

Ministering To Youth

Selected Sermons (Vol. I-X)

(Christian School Materials)

****

Copyright ©1989
by Dr. Samuel C. Gipp
4th Printing -- 1996
5th Printing – 1999
6th Printing – 2001
7th Printing – 2003

ISBN 1-890120-00-6

Printed by
Bible & Literature Missionary Foundation
713 Cannon Blvd., Shelbyville, TN 37160

Dedication

This Book is Dedicated to:

First, the belief that ''The Bible is our final authority in all matters of faith and practice.''

Second, to the common man who has been bullied and intimidated into believing that the Bible has errors in it.

Third, to Tom, a young man I knew years ago who had his faith in the infallible Bible destroyed by his Bible college education. Only to be replaced by contempt for those who still believe it.

Contents

Preface

The Reason for This Book

The reason for this book is two-fold.

First, it was written to answer the raft of questions used by critics of the King James Bible to attack and destroy the faith of anyone who really BELIEVES that the Bible is infallible. The style is such that its arguments can be understood and advanced by one who has NOT had the benefit (or curse) of a Bible college education.

This brings us to the second reason for its existence. Some time ago a leader of a large fundamental movement made the statement, "What really fires me is...these guys with a High School education debating textual criticism."

That is the second purpose of this book. For years those faithful folk who have not been to college have been bullied around for their lack of formal education by an arm load of D.D.'s who seek to keep them "in the dark." Many of these people have done more serious study of the Bible issue in the privacy of their homes than the honorarily doctored critics have in college classrooms. Yet the common man is often intimidated by the "trick" questions asked by his "educated" foe. The critic feels invincible in his armor of education.

This book is written so that the ordinary Christian will be properly equipped to defend him or herself from the fiery darts of their pompous foes.

In fact, they may even punch a few holes in their armor.

Author's Note

All reference to "the Bible," "the Holy Bible," "God's Perfect Bible," "Holy Scripture," etc, are references to the Authorized Version of 1611, also known as the King James Bible, unless otherwise defined by the immediate context of a passage.

Also: Although each question is handled individually, some of the later questions build on the answer of a previous question. For that reason it is advisable to read this book from start to finish rather than by skipping around to the questions that most interest you.

Thank you,

Dr. Samuel C. Gipp

Question #1

QUESTION: Shouldn't we be loyal to the "original autographs" and not a mere translation?

ANSWER: We should put as much value on the "originals" as God does.

EXPLANATION: It is impossible to be true to the originals because the originals have long been lost. This **well established fact** should be enough to make the sincere student of Scripture realize that an affirmative answer to the question is an impossibility.

But it does not explain the above answer. Just how much value **does** God put on the originals?

To get the answer we must explore several chapters in the book of Jeremiah beginning with the famous passage in chapter 36 concerning the roll that Jeremiah had written.

In verse 21 the roll is brought before King Jehoiakim and read by his servant Jehudi.

According to verse 23 Jehudi read three or four leaves and King Jehoiakim cut it up with a penknife and cast it into the fire on the hearth until it was destroyed.

Thus ends ORIGINAL #1 !

Then the Lord moved Jeremiah to rewrite the roll adding some words to it. (Jeremiah 36:32)

Thus ORIGINAL #2 is born.

We are shown the text of this second original in Jeremiah 45-51 where it is reproduced for our benefit.

Jeremiah told Seraiah to read this roll when he came into

Babylon. (Jeremiah 51:59-61) Then Jeremiah instructed Seraiah, after he finished reading the roll, to **bind a stone to it and cast it into the Euphrates river** (Jeremiah 51:63)!

Thus ends ORIGINAL #2!

But wait! We have a copy of the text of the roll in chapters 45-51. Were did it come from? It came from a **copy** of original #2 which we can only call ORIGINAL #3!

So there are two very big problems for those who overemphasize the ''originals''.

(1) Every Bible ever printed with a copy of Jeremiah in it has a text in chapters 45-51 which is translated from a copy of the ''second'' original, or ORIGINAL #3.

(2) Secondly, NO ONE can overlook the fact that God didn't have the **least** bit of interest in **preserving** the ''original'' once it had been copied and it's message delivered. So WHY should we put more of an emphasis on the originals than **God** does? An emphasis which is **plainly** unscriptural.

Thus, since we have the text of the ''originals'' preserved in the King James Bible we have no need of the originals, even if they **were** available.

Question #2

QUESTION: Isn't "Easter in Acts 12:4 a mistranslation of the word "pascha" and should it be translated as "passover"?

ANSWER: No, "pascha" is properly translated "Easter" in Acts 12:4 as the following explanation will show.

EXPLANATION: The Greek word which is translated "Easter" in Acts 12:4 is the word "pascha". This word appears twenty-nine times in the New Testament. Twenty-eight of those times the word is rendered "passover" in reference to the night when the Lord passed over Egypt and killed all the firstborn of Egypt (Exodus 12:12), thus setting Israel free from four hundred years of bondage.

The many opponents to the concept of having a perfect Bible have made much of this translation of "pascha".

Coming to the word "Easter" in God's Authorized Bible, they seize upon it imagining that they have found proof that the Bible is not perfect. Fortunately for lovers of the word of God, they are wrong. Easter, as we know it, comes from the ancient pagan festival of Astarte. Also known as Ishtar (pronounced "Easter"). This festival has always been held late in the month of April. It was, in it's original form, a celebration of the earth "regenerating" itself after the winter season. The festival involved a celebration of **reproduction**. For this reason the common symbols of Easter festivities were the **rabbit** (the same symbol as "Playboy" magazine), and the **egg**. **Both** are known for their reproductive abilities. At the center of attention was Astarte, the female deity. She is known in the Bible as the "queen of heaven" (Jeremiah 7:18; 44:17-25). She is the **mother** of Tammuz (Ezekiel 8:14) who was also her **husband!** These perverted rituals would take place at sunrise on Easter morning (Ezekiel 8:13-16). From the references in Jeremiah and Ezekiel, we can see that the true Easter has **never** had **any** association with Jesus Christ.

Problem: Even though the Jewish passover was held in mid April (the fourteenth) and the pagan festival Easter was held later the same month, **how** do we know that Herod was referring to Easter in Acts 12:4 and not the Jewish passover? If he was referring to the passover, the translation of "pascha" as "Easter" is incorrect. If he was indeed referring to the pagan holyday (holiday) Easter, then the King James Bible (1611) must truly be the very word and words of God for it is the only Bible in print today which has the correct reading.

To unravel the confusion concerning "Easter" in verse 4, we must consult our **FINAL** authority, **THE BIBLE.** The key which unlocks the puzzle is found **not** in verse 4, but in verse 3. (**Then** were the days of unleavened bread...") To secure the answer that we seek, we must find the relationship of the passover to the days of unleavened bread. We must keep in mind that Peter was arrested **during** the "days of unleavened bread" (Acts 12:3).

Our investigation will need to start at the **first** passover. This was the night in which the LORD smote all the firstborn in Egypt. The Israelites were instructed to kill a lamb and strike its blood on the two side posts and the upper door post (Exodus 12:4,5). Let us now see what the Bible says concerning the first passover, and the days of unleavened bread.

Exodus 12:13-18: *"And the blood shall be to you for a token upon the houses where ye are: and when I see the blood, I will pass over you, and the plague shall not be upon you to destroy you, when I smite the land of Egypt.*

*14 And **this day** shall be unto you for a memorial; and ye shall keep it a feast to the LORD throughout your generations; ye shall keep it a feast by an ordinance for ever.*

*15 **Seven days** shall ye eat unleavened bread; even the first day ye shall put away leaven out of your houses: for whoso-*

4

ever eateth leavened bread from the first day until the seventh day, that soul shall be cut off from Israel.

16 And in the first day there shall be an holy convocation to you; no manner of work shall be done in them, save that which every man must eat, that only may be done of you.

17 And ye shall observe the feast of unleavened bread; for in this selfsame day have I brought your armies out of the land of Egypt: therefore shall ye observe this day in your generations by an ordinance for ever.

*18 **In the first month, on the fourteenth day of the month at even,** ye shall eat unleavened bread, until the one and twentieth day of the month at even."*

Here in Exodus 12:13 we see how the passover got its name. The LORD said that He would "pass over" all of the houses which had the blood of the lamb marking the door.

After the passover (Exodus 12:13,14), we find that seven days shall be fulfilled in which the Jews were to eat unleavened bread. **These** are the days of unleavened bread!

In verse 18 we see that dates for the observance were April 14th through the 21st.

This religious observance is stated more clearly in **Numbers 28:16-18:** *"And in the fourteenth day of the first month is the passover of the LORD.*

17 And in the fifteenth day of this month is the feast: seven days shall unleavened bread be eaten.

18 In the first day shall be an holy convocation; ye shall do no manner of servile work therein:"

In verse 16 we see that the passover is only considered to be the 14th of the month. On the next morning, the 15th begins the "days of unleavened bread."

Deuteronomy 16:1-8: *"Observe the **month of Abib** (April), and keep the passover unto the LORD thy God: for in the month of Abib the LORD thy God brought thee forth out of Egypt by night.*

2 Thou shalt therefore sacrifice the passover unto the LORD thy God, of the flock and the herd, in the place which the LORD shall choose to place his name there.

*3 Thou shalt eat no leavened bread with it; **seven days shalt thou eat unleavened bread therewith,** even the bread of*

5

affliction: for thou camest forth out of the land of Egypt in haste :that thou mayest remember the day when thou camest forth out of the land of Egypt all the days of thy life.

4 And there shall be no leavened bread seen with thee in all thy coast seven days; neither shall there any thing of the flesh, which thou sacrificedst the first day at even, remain all night until the morning.

5 Thou mayest not sacrifice the passover within any of thy gates, which the LORD thy God giveth thee:

6 But at the place which the LORD thy God shall choose to place his name in, there thou shalt sacrifice the passover at even, at the going down of the sun, at the season that thou camest forth out of Egypt.

7 And thou shalt roast and eat it in the place which the LORD thy God shall choose: and thou shalt turn in the morning, and go unto thy tents.

8 Six days thou shalt eat unleavened bread: and on the seventh day shall be a solemn assembly to the LORD thy God: thou shalt do no work therein.''

Here in Deuteronomy we see again that the passover is sacrificed on the **first** night (Deuteronomy 16:1). It is worth noting that the passover was to be celebrated in the evening (vs.6) **not** at sunrise (Ezekiel 8:13-16).

In II Chronicles 8:13 we see that the feast of unleavened bread was one of the three Jewish feasts to be kept during the year.

II Chronicles 8:13: *''Even after a certain rate every day, offering according to the commandment of Moses, on the sabbaths, and on the new moons, and on the solemn feasts, three times in the year, even in the feast of unleavened bread, and in the feast of weeks, and in the feust of tabernacles.''*

Whenever the passover was kept, it **always** preceded the feast of unleavened bread. In II Chronicles 30 some Jews who were unable to keep the passover in the **first** month were allowed to keep it in the second. But the **dates** remained the same.

II Chronicles 30:15,21: *''Then they killed the passover on the fourteenth day of the second month: and the priests and the Levites were ashamed, and sanctified themselves, and* *brought in the burnt offerings into the house of the LORD. And the children of Israel that were present at Jerusalem kept the feast of unleavened bread seven days with great gladness: and the Levites and the priests praised the LORD day by day, singing with loud instruments unto the LORD.''*

Ezra 6:19,22: *''And the children of the captivity kept the passover upon the fourteenth day of the first month. And kept the feast of unleavened bread seven days with joy: for the LORD had made them joyful, and turned the heart of the king of Assyria unto them, to strengthen their hands in the work of the house of God, the God of Israel.''*

We see then, from studying what the **BIBLE** has to say concerning the subject that the order of events went as follows:

(1) On the 14th of April the lamb was killed. **This** is the passover. No event following the 14th is ever referred to as the passover.

(2) On the morning of the 15th begins the days of unleavened bread, also known as the feast of unleavened bread.

It must also be noted that whenever the passover is mentioned in the New Testament, the reference is **always** to the meal, to be eaten on the night of April 14th **not** the entire week. The days of unleavened bread are NEVER referred to as the passover. (It must be remembered that the angel of the Lord passed over Egypt on **one** night, **not** seven nights in a row.

Now let us look at **Acts 12:3,4:** *''And because he saw it pleased the Jews, he proceeded further to take Peter also. (Then were the days of unleavened bread.) And when he had apprehended him, he put him in prison, and delivered him to four quaternions of soldiers to keep him; intending after Easter to bring him forth to the people.''*

Verse 3 shows that Peter was arrested during the days of unleavened bread (April 15-21). The Bible says: ''**Then** were the days of unleavened bread.'' The passover (April 14th) had **already come and gone.** Herod could not possibly have been referring to the passover in his statement concerning Easter. The next passover was a **year away!** But the pagan holiday of Easter was just a **few days away.** Remember! Herod was a pagan Roman who worshipped the "queen of heaven". He was **NOT** a Jew. He had no reason to keep the Jewish passover. Some might argue that he wanted to wait until after the passover for fear of upsetting the Jews. There are two grievous faults in this line of thinking.

First, Peter was no longer considered a Jew. He had repudiated Judaism. The Jews would have no reason to be upset by Herod's actions.

Second, he could not have been waiting until after the passover because he thought the Jews would not kill a man during a religious holiday. They had killed **Jesus** during passover (Matthew 26:17-19,47). They were also excited about Herod's murder of James. Anyone knows that a mob possesses the courage to do violent acts **during** religious festivities, not after.

In further considering Herod's position as a Roman, we must remember that the Herod's were well known for celebrating (Matthew 14:6-11). In fact, in Matthew chapter 14 we see that a Herod was even willing to kill a man of God during one of his celebrations.

It is elementary to see that Herod, in Acts 12, had arrested Peter during the days of unleavened bread, **after the passover**. The days of unleavened bread would end on the 21st of April. Shortly after that would come Herod's celebration of pagan Easter. Herod had not killed Peter during the days of unleavened bread simply because he wanted to wait until **Easter**. Since it is plain that both the Jews (Matthew 26:17-47) and the Romans (Matthew 14:6-11) would kill during a religious celebration, Herod's opinion seemed that he was not going to let the Jews "have all the fun". He would wait until his own pagan festival and see to it that Peter died in the excitement.

Thus we see that it was God's providence which had the Spirit-filled translators of our Bible (King James) to **CORRECTLY** translate "pascha" as "Easter". It most certainly did not refer to the Jewish passover. In fact, to change it to "passover" would confuse the reader and make the truth of the situation unclear.

Question #3

QUESTION: I have been told that King James was a homosexual. Is this true?

ANSWER: No.

EXPLANATION: King James I of England, who authorized the translation of the now famous King James Bible, was considered by many to be one of the greatest, if not the greatest, monarchs that England has ever seen.

Through his wisdom and determination he united the warring tribes of Scotland into a unified nation, and then joined England and Scotland to form the foundation for what is now known as the British Empire.

At a time when only the churches of England possessed the Bible in English, King James' desire was that the common people should have the Bible in their native tongue. Thus, in 1603, King James called 54 of history's most learned men together to accomplish this great task. At a time when the leaders of the world wished to keep their subjects in spiritual ignorance, King James offered his subjects the greatest gift that he could give them. Their own copy of the Word of God in English.

James, who was fluent in Latin, Greek, and French, and schooled in Italian and Spanish even wrote a tract entitled ''Counterblast to Tobacco'', which was written to help thwart the use of tobacco in England.

Such a man was sure to have enemies. One such man, Anthony Weldon, had to be excluded from the court. Weldon swore vengeance. It was not until 1650, **twenty-five years after the death of James** that Weldon saw his chance. He wrote a paper calling James a homosexual. Obviously, James, being dead, was in no condition to defend himself.

The report was largely ignored since there were still enough people alive who knew it wasn't true. In fact, it lay dormant for years, until recently when it was picked up by Christians who hoped that vilifying King James, would tarnish the Bible that bears his name so that Christians would turn away from God's book to a more "modern" translation.

It seems though, that Weldon's false account is being once again largely ignored by the majority of Christianity with the exception of those with an ulterior motive, such as its author had.

It might also be mentioned here that the Roman Catholic Church was so desperate to keep the true Bible out of the hands of the English people that it attempted to kill King James and all of Parliament in 1605.

In 1605 a Roman Catholic by the name of Guy Fawkes, under the direction of a Jesuit priest by the name of Henry Garnet, was found in the basement of Parliament with thirty-six barrels of gunpowder which he was to use to blow up King James and the entire Parliament. After killing the king, they planned on imprisoning his children, re-establishing England as a state loyal to the Pope and kill all who resisted. Needless to say, the perfect English Bible would have been one of the plot's victims. Fawkes and Garnet and eight other conspirators were caught and hanged.

It seems that those who work so hard to discredit the character of King James join an unholy lot.

Question #4

QUESTION: Aren't there archaic words in the Bible, and don't we need a modern translation to eliminate them?

ANSWER: Yes and No. Yes there are archaic words in the Bible but No, we do not need a modern translation to eliminate them.

EXPLANATION: That there are archaic words in the Bible is very true. An archaic word is a word which is no longer used in every day speech and has been replaced by another. A good example of an archaic word is found in I Corinthians 10:25.

"Whatsoever is sold in the shambles, that eat, asking no question for conscience sake:"

The word "shambles" is archaic. It has been replaced in common speech with the word "market place". Indeed we can be certain that "shambles" was a much more accurate description of the ancient market place (and many around the world today). It has none the less passed from common use.

Well then, shouldn't we publish a new translation which removes "shambles" and inserts the more common "market place"?

No, what we **should** do is turn to the Bible, our final authority in all matters of **faith** and **practice** and see what the Bible **practice** is concerning archaic words. For surely we believers in a perfect Bible will want to follow the **Bible's** practice concerning archaic words.

In searching the Scripture we find the Bible **practice** for handling archaic words in I Samuel chapter 9:1-11. *"Now there was a man of Benjamin, whose name was Kish, the son of Zeror, the son of Bechorath, the son of Aphiah, a Benjamite,a mighty man of power.*

2 And he had a son, whose name was Saul, a choice young man, and a goodly: and there was not among the children of Israel a goodlier person than he: from his shoulders and upward he was higher than any of the people.

3 And the asses of Kish Saul's father were lost. And Kish said to Saul his son, Take now one of the servants with thee, and arise, go seek the asses.

4 And he passed through mount Ephraim, and passed through the land of Shalisha, but they found them not: then they passed through the land of Shalim, and there they were not: and he passed through the land of the Benjamites, but they found them not.

5 And when they were come to the land of Zuph, Saul said to his servant that was with him, Come, and let us return; lest my father leave caring for the asses, and take thought for us.

6 And he said unto him, Behold now, there is in this city a man of God, and he is an honourable man; all that he saith cometh surely to pass: now let us go thither; peradventure he can shew us our way that we should go.

7 Then said Saul to his servant, But, behold, if we go, what shall we bring the man? for the bread is spent in our vessels, and there is not a present to bring to the man of God: what have we?

8 And the servant answered Saul again, and said, Behold, I have here at hand the fourth part of a shekel of silver: that will I give to the man of God, to tell us our way.

9 (Beforetime in Israel, when a man went to inquire of God, thus he spake, Come, and let us go to the seer: for he that is now called a Prophet was beforetime called a Seer.)

10 Then said Saul to his servant, Well said; come let us go. So they went unto the city where the man of God was.

11 And as they went up the hill to the city, they found young maidens going out to draw water, and said unto them, Is the seer here?"

Here, in the first eleven verses of I Samuel 9 we are not only confronted with an archaic word, but with the Bible **practice** for handling it.

We find Saul and one of his father's servants searching for the asses that had run off (I Samuel 9:1-5). They decide to go to see Samuel the seer and enlist his help in finding the asses (verses 6-8).

In verse 11 we are going to run into an archaic word. But, before we do, God puts a parenthesis in the narrative (verse 9) to tell us about it. Notice that verse 9 states that "he that is now called a **Prophet** was beforetime called a **Seer**". Thus we see that, between the time that this event took place and the time that the incident was divinely recorded the word "Seer" had passed from common use to be replaced with "Prophet". "Seer" was now archaic.

BUT, look carefully at **verse 11** where the archaic word appeared.

"And as they went up the hill to the city, they found young maidens going out to draw water, and said unto them, Is the **seer** here?"

Please note that the verse **retains** the outdated word "seer". It does **not** say "Is the prophet here?".

Thus we see that **God Himself** through the **divine inspiration** of the Holy Spirit used verse 9 to **explain** the upcoming archaic word but **did not change the holy text!**

So we see that, the **Bible practice** for handling situations such as we find in I Corinthians 10:25 when preaching is to tell the congregation something to the effect that "What beforetime was called 'shambles' is now called 'market place'". But **we should leave the archaic word in the text. This is what God did!** Surely we sinners are not going to come up with a better method for handling archaic words than God has.

So, the answer to the question is, "Yes, there are archaic words in the Bible but **No** we do not need a modern translation to eliminate them. **God** didn't change His Book, He certainly does not want **us** doing it.

Question #5

QUESTION: Haven't there been several revisions of the King James Bible since 1611?

ANSWER: No. There have been several editions but no revisions.

EXPLANATION: One of the last ditch defenses of a badly shaken critic of the Authorized Version 1611 is the "revision hoax." They run to this seeming fortress in an attempt to stave off ultimate defeat by their opponents who overwhelm their feeble arguments with historic facts, manuscript evidence and to obvious workings of the Holy Spirit. Once inside, they turn self-confidently to their foes and ask with a smug look, "Which King James do you use, the 1611 or the 1629 or perhaps the 1769?" The shock of this attack and the momentary confusion that results usually allows them time to make good their escape.

Unfortunately, upon entering their castle and closing the door behind them they find that their fortress has been systematically torn down, brick by brick, by a man with the title of Dr. David F. Reagan.

Dr. Reagan pastors the Trinity Baptist Temple in Knoxville, Tennessee. He has written a devastating expose' on the early editions of the King James Bible entitled "The King James Version of 1611. The Myth of Early Revisions."

Dr. Reagan has done an excellent job of destroying the last stronghold of Bible critics. I see neither a way, nor a reason to try to improve on his finding. So I have secured his permission to reproduce his pamphlet in its entirety.

THE KING JAMES VERSION OF 1611
THE MYTH OF EARLY REVISIONS

Introduction

Men have been "handling the word of God deceitfully" (II Cor. 4:2) ever since the devil first taught Eve how. From Cain to Balaam, from Jehudi to the scribes and Pharisees, from the Dark Age theologians to present-day scholars, the living words of the Almighty God have been prime targets for man's corrupting hand. The attacks on the Word of God are three-fold: addition, subtraction, and substitution. From Adam's day to the computer age, the strategies have remained the same. There is nothing new under the sun.

One attack which is receiving quite a bit of attention these days is a direct attack on the Word of God as preserved in the English language: the King James Version of 1611. The attack referred to is the myth which claims that since the King James Version has already been revised four times, there should be and can be no valid objection to other revisions. This myth was used by the English Revisers of 1881 and has been revived in recent years by Fundamentalist scholars hoping to sell their latest translation. This book is given as an answer to this attack. The purpose of the material is not to convince those who would deny this preservation but to strengthen the faith of those who already believe in a pre-served English Bible.

One major question often arises in any attack such as this. How far should we go in answering the critics? If we were to attempt to answer every shallow objection to the infallibility of the English Bible, we would never be able to accomplish anything else. Sanity must prevail somewhere. As always, the answer is in God's Word. Proverbs 26:4-5 states: Answer not a fool according to his folly, lest thou also be like unto him. Answer a fool according to his folly, lest he be wise in his own conceit.

Obviously, there are times when a foolish query should be

15

ignored and times when it should be met with an answer. If to answer the attack will make you look as foolish as the attacker, then the best answer is to ignore the question. For instance, if you are told that the Bible cannot be infallible because so-and-so believes that it is, and he is divorced, then you may safely assume that silence is the best answer. On the other hand, there are often questions and problems that, if true, would be serious. To ignore these issues would be to leave the Bible attacker wise in his own conceit. I believe that the question of revisions to the King James Version of 1611 is a question of the second class. If the King James Version has undergone four major revisions of its text, then to oppose further revisions on the basis of an established English text would truly be faulty. For this reason, this attack should and must be answered. Can the argument be answered? Certainly! That is the purpose of this book.

I - THE PRINTING CONDITIONS OF 1611

If God did preserve His Word in the English language through the Authorized Version of 1611 (and He did), then where is our authority for the infallible wording? Is it in the notes of the translators? Or is it to be found in the proof copy sent to the printers? If so, then our authority is lost because these papers are lost. But, you say, the authority is in the first copy which came off the printing press. Alas, that copy has also certainly perished. In fact, if the printing of the English Bible followed the pattern of most printing jobs, the first copy was probably discarded because of bad quality. That leaves us with existing copies of the first printing. They are the ones often pointed out as the standard by which all other King James Bibles are to be compared. But are they? Can those early printers of the first edition not be allowed to make printing errors? We need to establish one thing from the outset. The authority for our preserved English text is not found in any human work. The authority for our preserved and infallible English text is in God! Printers may foul up at times and humans will still make plenty of errors, but God in His power and mercy will preserve His text despite the weaknesses of fallible man. Now, let us look at the pressures on a printer in the year of 1611.

Although the printing press had been invented in 1450 by Johann Gutenburg in Germany (161 years before the 1611 printing), the equipment used by the printer had changed very little. Printing was still very slow and difficult. All type was set by hand, one piece at a time (that's one piece at a time through the whole Bible), and errors were an expected part of any completed book. Because of this difficulty and also because the 1611 printers had no earlier editions from which to profit, the very first edition of the King James Version had a number of printing errors. As shall later be demonstrated, these were not the sort of textual alterations which are freely made in modern bibles. They were simple, obvious printing errors of the sort that can still be found at times in recent editions even with all of the advantages of modern printing. These errors do not render a Bible useless, but they should be corrected in later editions.

The two original printings of the Authorized Version demonstrate the difficulty of printing in 1611 without making mistakes. Both editions were printed in Oxford. Both were printed in the same year: 1611. The same printers did both jobs. Most likely, both editions were printed on the same printing press. Yet, in a strict comparison of the two editions, approximately 100 textual differences can be found. In the same vein the King James critics can find only about 400 alleged textual alterations in the King James Version after 375 years of printing and four so-called revisions! Something is rotten in Scholarsville! The time has come to examine these "revisions."

II - THE FOUR SO-CALLED REVISIONS OF THE 1611 KJV

Much of the information in this section is taken from a book by F.H.A. Scrivener called The Authorized Edition of the English Bible (1611), Its Subsequent Reprints and Modern Representatives. The book is as pedantic as its title indicates. The interesting point is that Scrivener, who published this book in 1884, was a member of the Revision Committee of 1881. He was not a King James Bible believer, and therefore his material is not biased toward the Authorized Version.

In the section of Scrivener's book dealing with the KJV "revisions," one initial detail is striking. The first two so-called major revisions of the King James Bible occurred within 27 years of the original printing. (The language must have been changing very rapidly in those days.) The 1629 edition of the Bible printed in Cambridge is said to have been the first revision. A revision it was not, but simply a careful correction of earlier printing errors. Not only was this edition completed just eighteen years after the translation, but two of the men who participated in this printing, Dr. Samuel Ward and John Bois, had worked on the original translation of the King James Version. Who better to correct early errors than two who had worked on the original translation! Only nine years later and in Cambridge again, another edition came out which is supposed to have been the second major revision. Both Ward and Bois were still alive, but it is not known if they participated at this time. But even Scrivener, who as you remember worked on the English Revised Version of 1881, admitted that the Cambridge printers had simply reinstated words and clauses overlooked by the 1611 printers and amended manifest errors. According to a study which will be detailed later, 72% of the approximately 400 textual corrections in the KJV were completed by the time of the 1638 Cambridge edition, only 27 years after the original printing!

Just as the first two so-called revisions were actually two stages of one process: the purification of early printing errors, so the last two so-called revisions were two stages in another process: the standardization of the spelling. These two editions were only seven years apart (1762 and 1769) with the second one completing what the first had started. But when the scholars are numbering revisions, two sounds better than one. Very few textual corrections were necessary at this time. The thousands of alleged changes are spelling changes made to match the established correct forms. These spelling changes will be discussed later. Suffice it to say at this time that the tale of four major revisions is truly a fraud and a myth. But you say, there are still changes whether they be few or many. What are you going to do with the changes that are still there? Let us now examine the character of these changes.

III - THE SO-CALLED THOUSANDS
OF CHANGES

Suppose someone were to take you to a museum to see an original copy of the King James Version. You come to the glass case where the Bible is displayed and look down at the opened Bible through the glass. Although you are not allowed to flip through its pages, you can readily tell that there are some very different things about this Bible from the one you own. You can hardly read its words, and those you can make out are spelled in odd and strange ways. Like others before you, you leave with the impression that the King James Version has undergone a multitude of changes since its original printing in 1611. But beware, you have just been taken by a very clever ploy. The differences you saw are not what they seem to be. Let's examine the evidence.

Printing Changes

For proper examination, the changes can be divided into three kinds: printing changes, spelling changes, and textual changes. Printing changes will be considered first. The type style used in 1611 by the KJV translators was the Gothic Type Style. The type style you are reading right now and are familiar with is Roman Type. Gothic Type is sometimes called Germanic because it originated in Germany. Remember, that is where printing was invented. The Gothic letters were formed to resemble the hand-drawn manuscript lettering of the Middle Ages. At first, it was the only style in use. The Roman Type Style was invented fairly early, but many years passed before it became the predominate style in most European countries. Gothic continued to be used in Germany until recent years. In 1611 in England, Roman Type was already very popular and would soon supersede the Gothic. However, the original printers chose the Gothic Style for the

KJV because it was considered to be more beautiful and eloquent than the Roman. But the change to Roman Type was not long in coming. In 1612, the first King James Version using Roman Type was printed. Within a few years, all the bibles printed used the Roman Type Style.

Please realize that a change in type style no more alters the text of the Bible than a change in format or type size does. However, the modern reader who has not become familiar with Gothic can find it very difficult to understand. Besides some general change in form, several specific letter changes need to be observed. For instance, the **Gothic s** looks like the **Roman s** when used as a capital letter or at the end of a word. But when it is used as a lower case **s** at the beginning or in the middle of a word, the letter looks like our **f**. Therefore, **also** becomes **alfo** and **set** becomes **fet**. Another variation is found in the **German v** and **u**. The **Gothic v** looks like a **Roman u** while the **Gothic u** looks like the **Roman v**. This explains why our **w** is called a double-u and not a double-v. Sound confusing? It is until you get used to it. In the 1611 edition, **love** is **loue**, **us** is **vs**, and **ever** is **euer**. But remember, these are not even spelling changes. They are simply type style changes. In another instance, the **Gothic j** looks like our **i**. So **Jesus** becomes **Iefus** (notice the middle **s** changed to **f**) and **joy** becomes **ioy**. Even the **Gothic d** with the stem leaning back over the circle in a shape resembling that of the **Greek Delta**. These changes account for a large percentage of the "thousands" of changes in the KJV, yet they do no harm whatsoever to the text. They are nothing more than a smokescreen set up by the attackers of our English Bible.

Spelling Changes

Another kind of change found in the history of the Authorized Version are changes of orthography or spelling. Most histories date the beginning of Modern English around the year 1500. Therefore, by 1611 the grammatical structure and basic vocabulary of present-day English had long been established. However, the spelling did not stabilize at the same time. In the 1600's spelling was according to whim. There was no such thing as correct spelling. No standards had been established. An author often spelled the same word several different ways, often in the same book and sometimes on the same page. And these were the educated people. Some of you reading this today would have found the 1600's a spelling paradise. Not until the eighteenth century did the spelling begin to take a stable form. Therefore, in the last half of the eighteenth century, the spelling of the King James Version of 1611 was standardized.

What kind of spelling variations can you expect to find between your present edition and the 1611 printing? Although every spelling difference cannot be categorized, several characteristics are very common. Additional **e's** were often found at the end of the words such as **feare, darke**, and **beare**. Also, double vowels were much more common than they are today. You would find **ee, bee**, and **mooued** instead of **me, be**, and **moved**. Double consonants were also much more common. What would **ranne, euill**, and **ftarres** be according to present-day spelling? See if you can figure them out. The present-day spellings would be **ran, evil**, and **stars**. These typographical and spelling changes account for almost all of the so-called thousands of changes in the King James Bible. None of them alter the text in any way. Therefore they cannot be honestly compared with thousands of true textual changes which are blatantly made in the modern versions.

Textual Changes

Almost all of the alleged changes have been accounted for. We now come to the question of actual textual differences between our present editions and that of 1611. There are some differences between the two, but they are not the changes of a revision. They are instead the correction of early printing errors. That this is a fact may be seen in three things: (1) the character of the changes, (2) the frequency of the changes throughout the Bible, and (3) the time the changes were made. First, let us look at the character of the changes made from the time of the first printing of the Authorized English Bible.

The changes from the 1611 edition that are admittedly textual are obviously printing errors because of the nature of these changes. They are not textual changes made to alter the reading. In the first printing, words were sometimes inverted. Sometimes a plural was written as singular or visa versa. At times a word was miswritten for one that was similar. A few times a word or even a phrase was omitted. The omissions were obvious and did not have the doctrinal implications of those found in modern translations. If fact, there is really no comparison between the corrections made in the King James text and those proposed by the scholars of today.

F.H.A. Scrivener, in the appendix of his book, lists the variations between the 1611 edition of the KJV and later printings. A sampling of these corrections is given below. In order to be objective, the samples give the first textual correction on consecutive left hand pages of Scrivener's book. The 1611 reading is given first; then the present reading; and finally, the date the correction was first made.

1 this thing - this thing also *(1638)*
2 shalt have remained - ye shall have remained *(1762)*
3 Achzib, nor Helbath, nor Aphik - of Achzib, nor of Helbath, nor of Aphik *(1762)*
4 requite good - requite me good *(1629)*
5 this book of the Covenant - the book of this covenant *(1629)*
6 chief rulers - chief ruler *(1629)*
7 And Parbar - At Parbar *(1638)*
8 For this cause - And for this cause *(1638)*
9 For the king had appointed - for so the king had appointed *(1629)*
10 Seek good - seek God *(1617)*
11 The cormorant - But the cormorant *(1629)*
12 returned - turned *(1769)*
13 a fiery furnace - a burning fiery furnace *(1638)*
14 The crowned - Thy crowned *(1629)*
15 thy right doeth - thy right hand doeth *(1613)*
16 the wayes side - the way side *(1743)*
17 which was a Jew - which was a Jewess *(1629)*
18 the city - the city of the Damascenes *(1629)*
19 now and ever - both now and ever *(1638)*
20 which was of our father's - which was our fathers *(1616)*

Before your eyes are 5% of the textual changes made in the King James Version in 375 years. Even if they were not corrections of previous errors, they would be of no comparison to modern alterations. But they are corrections of printing errors, and therefore no comparison is at all possible. Look at the list for yourself and you will find only one that has serious doctrinal implications. In fact, in an examination of Scrivener's entire appendix, it is the only variation found by this author that could be accused of being doctrinal. I am referring to Psalm 69:32 where the 1611 edition has "seek good" when the Bible should have read "seek God." Yet, even with this error, two points demonstrate that this was indeed a printing error. First, the similarity of the words "good" and "God" in spelling shows how easily a weary typesetter could misread the proof and put the wrong word in the text. Second, this error was so obvious that it was caught and corrected in the year 1617, only six years after the original printing and well before the first so-called revision. The myth that there are several major revisions to the 1611 KJV should be getting clearer. But there is more.

Not only does the character of the changes show them to be printing errors, so does their frequency. Fundamentalist scholars refer to the thousands of revisions made to the 1611 as if they were on a par with the recent bible versions. They are not. The overwhelming majority of them are either type style or spelling changes. The few which do remain are clearly corrections of printing errors made because of the tediousness involved in the early printing process. The sample list given above will demonstrate just how careful Scrivener was in listing all the variations. Yet, even with this great care, only approximately 400 variations are named between the 1611 edition and modern copies. Remember that there were 100 variations between the first two Oxford editions which were both printed in 1611. Since there are almost 1200 chapters in the Bible, the average variation per chapter (after 375 years) is one third, i.e., one correction per every three chapters. These are changes such as "chief rulers" to "chief ruler" and "And Parbar" to "At Parbar." But there is yet one more evidence that these variations are simply corrected printing errors: the early date at which they were corrected.

The character and frequency of the textual changes clearly separate them from modern alterations. But the time the changes were made settles the issue absolutely. The great majority of the 400 corrections were made within a few years of the original printing. Take, for example, our earlier sampling. Of the twenty corrections listed, one was made in 1613, one in 1616, one in 1617, eight in 1629, five in 1638, one in 1743, two in 1762, and one in 1769. That means that 16 out of 20 corrections, or 80%, were made within twenty-seven years of the 1611 printing. That is hardly the long drawn out series of revisions the scholars would have you to believe. In another study made by examining every other page of Scrivener's appendix in detail, 72% of the textual corrections were made by 1638. There is no "revision" issue.

The character of the textual changes is that of obvious errors. The frequency of the textual changes is sparse, occurring only once per three chapters. The chronology of the textual changes is early with about three fourths of them occurring within twenty-seven years of the first printing. All of these details establish the fact that there were no true revisions in the sense of updating the language or correcting translation errors. There were only editions which corrected early typographical errors. Our source of authority for the exact wording of the 1611 Authorized Version is not in the existing copies of the first printing. Our source of authority for the exact wording of our English Bible is in the preserving power of Almighty God. Just as God did not leave us the original autographs to fight and squabble over, so He did not see fit to leave us the proof copy of the translation. Our authority is in the hand of God as always. You can praise the Lord for that!

IV - CHANGES IN THE BOOK OF ECCLESIASTES

An in-depth study of the changes made in the book of Ecclesiastes would help to illustrate the principles stated above. The author is grateful to Dr. David Reese of Millbrook, Alabama, for his work in this area. By comparing a 1611 reprint of the original edition put out by Thomas Nelson & Sons with recent printing of the King James Version, Dr. Reese was able to locate four variations in the book of Ecclesiastes. The reference is given first; then the text of the Thomas Nelson 1611 reprint. This is followed by the reading of the present editions of the 1611 KJV and the date the change was made.

1 1:5 the place - his place *(1638)*
2 2:16 shall be - shall all be *(1629)*
3 8:17 out, yea further - out, yet he shall not find it; yea farther *(1629)*
4 11:17 thing is it - thing it is *(?)*

Several things should be noted about these changes. The last variation ("thing is it" to "thing it is") is not mentioned by Scrivener who was a very careful and accurate scholar. Therefore, this change may be a misprint in the Thomas Nelson reprint. That would be interesting. The corrected omission in chapter eight is one of the longest corrections of the original printing. But notice that it was corrected in 1629. The frequency of printing errors is average (four errors in twelve chapters). But the most outstanding fact is that the entire book of Ecclesiastes reads exactly like our present editions without even printing errors by the year 1638. That's approximately 350 years ago. By that time, the Bible was being printed in Roman type. Therefore, all (and I mean all) that has changed in 350 years in the book of Ecclesiastes is that the spelling has been standardized! As stated before, the main purpose of the 1629 and 1638 Cambridge editions was the correction of earlier printing errors. And the main purpose of the 1762 and 1769 editions was the standardization of spelling.

V - THE SO-CALLED JUSTIFICATION
FOR OTHER REVISIONS

Maybe now you see that the King James Version of 1611 has not been revised but only corrected. But why does it make that much difference? Although there are several reasons why this issue is important, the most pressing one is that fundamentalist scholars are using this myth of past revisions to justify their own tampering with the text. The editors of the New King James Version have probably been the worst in recent years to use this propaganda ploy. In the preface of the New King James they have stated, "For nearly four hundred years, and throughout several revisions of its English form, the King James Bible has been deeply revered among the English-speaking peoples of the world." In the midst of their flowery rhetoric, they strongly imply that their edition is only a continuation of the revisions that have been going on for the past 375 years. This implication, which has been stated directly by others, could not be more false. To prove this point, we will go back to the book of Ecclesiastes.

An examination of the first chapter in Ecclesiastes in the New King James Version reveals approximately 50 changes from our present edition. In order to be fair, spelling changes (**cometh** to **comes**; **labour** to **labor**; etc.) were not included in this count. That means there are probably about 600 alterations in the book of Ecclesiastes and approximately 60,000 changes in the entire Bible. If you accuse me of including every recognizable change, you are correct. But I am only counting the sort of changes which were identified in analyzing the 1611 King James. That's only fair. Still, the number of changes is especially baffling for a version which claims to be an updating in the same vein as earlier revisions. According to the fundamentalist scholar, the New King James is only a fifth in a series of revisions. Then pray tell me how four "revisions" and 375 years brought only 400 changes while the fifth revision brought about 60,000 additional changes? That means that the fifth revision made 150 times more changes than the total number of changes in the first four! That's preposterous!

Not only is the frequency of the changes unbelievable, but the character of the alterations are serious. Although many of the alterations seem harmless enough at first glance, many are much more serious. The editors of the New King James Version were sly enough not to alter the most serious blunders of the modern bibles. Yet, they were not afraid to change the reading in those places that are unfamiliar to the average fundamentalist. In these areas, the New King James Version is dangerous. Below are some of the more harmful alterations made in the book of Ecclesiastes. The reference is given first; then the reading as found in the King James Version; and last, the reading as found in the New King James Version.

1:13   sore travail; grievous task
1:14   vexation of spirit; grasping for the wind
1:16   my heart had great experience of wisdom; My heart has understood great wisdom
 2:3   to give myself unto; to gratify my flesh with
 2:3   acquainting; guiding
2:21   equity; skill
3:10   the travail, which God hath given; the God-given task
3:11   the world; eternity
3:18   that God might manifest them; God tests them
3:18   they themselves are beasts; they themselves are like beasts
3:22   portion; heritage
 4:4   right work; skillful work
 5:1   Keep thy foot; Walk prudently
 5:6   the angel; the messenger of God
 5:6   thy voice   your excuse
 5:8   he that is higher than the highest; high official
5:20   God answereth him; God keeps him busy
 6:3   untimely birth; stillborn child
7:29   inventions; schemes
 8:1   boldness; sterness
8:10   the place of the holy; the place of holiness
10:1   Dead flies cause the ointment of the apothecary to send forth a stinking savour; Dead flies putrefy the perfumer's ointment
10:10 If the iron be blunt; If the ax is dull
10:10 wisdom is profitable to direct; wisdom brings success
12:9   gave good heed; pondered
12:11 the masters of assemblies; scholars

This is only a sampling of the changes in the book, but

notice what is done. Equity, which is a trait of godliness, becomes skill (2:21). The world becomes eternity (3:11). Man without God is no longer a beast but just like a beast (3:18). The clear reference to deity in Ecclesiastes 5:8 ("he that is higher than the highest") is successfully removed ("higher official"). But since success is what wisdom is supposed to bring us (10:10), this must be progress. At least God is keeping the scholars busy (5:20). Probably the most revealing of the above mentioned changes is the last one listed where "the masters of assemblies" become "scholars." According to the New King James, "the words of scholars are like well-driven nails, given by one Shepherd." The masters of assemblies are replaced by the scholars who become the source of the Shepherd's words. That is what these scholars would like us to think, but it is not true.

In conclusion, the New King James is not a revision in the vein of former revisions of the King James Version. It is instead an entirely new translation. As stated in the introduction, the purpose of this book is not to convince those who use the other versions. The purpose of this book is to expose a fallacious argument that has been circulating in fundamentalist circles for what it is: an overblown myth. That is, the myth that the New King James Version and others like it are nothing more than a continuation of revisions which have periodically been made to the King James Version since 1611. There is one problem with this theory. There are no such revisions.

The King James Bible of 1611 has not undergone four (or any) major revisions. Therefore, the New King James Version is not a continuation of what has gone on before. It should in fact be called the Thomas Nelson Version. They hold the copyright. The King James Version we have today has not been revised but purified. We still have no reason to doubt that the Bible we hold in our hands is the very word of God preserved for us in the English language. The authority for its veracity lies not in the first printing of the King James Version in 1611, or in the character of King James I, or in the scholarship of the 1611 translators, or in the literary accomplishments of Elizabethton England, or even in the Greek Received Text. Our authority for the infallible words of the

English Bible lies in the power and promise of God to preserve His Word! God has the power. We have His Word.

Individual copies of Dr. Reagan's excellent pamphlet can be obtained by sending one dollar to:

Trinity Baptist Temple Bookstore
5709 N. Broadway
Knoxville, Tennessee 37918
(615) 688-0780

Question #6

QUESTION: Don't the best manuscripts support the new versions?

ANSWER: No. The best manuscripts support the Bible, the Authorized Version.

EXPLANATION: The new versions are only supported by about five of the over 5,000 manuscripts of Bible text. Critics of the Bible claim that these manuscripts are better than those used by the translators of the Authorized Version. This is not so.

The two most prominent of these, Vaticanus, which is sole property of the Roman Catholic Church, and Sinaiticus are both known to be overwhelmed with errors. It is said that Sinaiticus has been corrected and altered by as many as ten different writers. In Vaticanus is found the evidence of very sloppy workmanship. Time and again words and whole phrases are repeated twice in succession or completely omitted. While the entire manuscript has had the text mutilated by some person or persons who ran over every letter with a pen making exact identification of many of the characters impossible.

Both manuscripts contain uninspired, anti-scriptural books which are not found in the Bible.

The only place where these error laden, unreliable manuscripts excel is in the quality of the materials used on them. They have good bindings and fine animal skin pages. Their physical appearance, contrary to their worthless texts, are really rather attractive. But then we have all heard the saying, "You can't tell a book by it's cover". The covers are beautiful but their texts are reprehensible.

And yet in spite of these well known corruptions, they are the basis for many new versions such as the New American Standard Version and the New International Version rendering these versions critically flawed and unreliable.

The manuscripts represented by the King James Bible have texts of the highest quality. So we see that the best manuscripts are those used by the King James translators.

Question #7

QUESTION: If there is a perfect Bible in English, doesn't there also have to be a perfect Bible in French, and German, and Japanese, etc?

ANSWER: No. God has always given His word to **one** people in **one** language to do **one** job; convert the world. The supposition that there must be a perfect translation in every language is erroneous and inconsistent with God's proven practice.

EXPLANATION: This explanation comes in three parts: the Old Testament, the New Testament, the entire Bible.

(1) The Old Testament:

It is an accepted fact that, with the exception of some portions of Ezra and Daniel, the Old Testament was written in Hebrew. It is also accepted that it was divinely given to the Jews.

Thus God initiates His pattern of operation. He gave His words to **one** people in only **one** language.

God, apparently unintimidated by modern scholarship, did not feel obligated to supply His words in Egyptian, Chaldian, Syrian, Ethiopian, or **any** other of the languages in use on the earth at the time the Old Testament was written.

The Old Testament was given **exclusively** to the Jews. Anyone desiring the word of God would have to convert to Judaism. Ample provision was made for such occurrences.

(2) New Testament:

It is also an accepted fact that the New Testament was

written in Greek. Koine Greek to be exact. Again, the Lord apparently saw no reason to inspire a perfect original in all of the languages of the world extant at that time.

Only this time, instead of giving His Book to a nation, such as Israel, He simply gave it to the Christians who were told to go out and convert the world. (Matthew 28:19) His choice of Greek as the language of the New Testament was obvious in that it was the predominant language of the world at the time.

(3) The Entire Bible:

It is obvious that God now needed to get both His Old Testament and His New Testament welded together in a language that was common to the world. Only English can be considered such a language.

The English language had been developing for many centuries until the late sixteenth century. About that time it finally reached a state of excellence that no language on earth has ever attained. It would seem that God did the rest. He chose this perfect language for the consummation of his perfect Book.

First England and later the United States swept the globe as the most powerful nations on earth, establishing English in all corners of the globe as either a primary or secondary language.

Today nations who do not speak English must still teach English to many of their citizens. Even nations antagonistic to the West such as Russia and Red China must teach English to their business and military personnel.

Thus in choosing English in which to combine His two Testaments, God chose the only language which the world would know. Just as He has shown in His choosing only **one** language for the Old Testament and only **one** language for the New Testament, He continued that practice by combining those two testaments in only **one** language.

But let us not forget the fact that, by choosing the English language, God has given us a **mandate** to carry out the great commission. He did not give us a perfect Bible to set placidly on the coffee table in our living room to let our guests know that we are "religious". He did not give it to us to press a flower from our first date, or to have a record of our family tree. He gave it to us to **read!** And to tuck under our arm and share with the lost world the good news of Jesus' payment for sin that is found inside.

Let's get busy!

Question #8

QUESTION: Where do Bible manuscripts come from?

ANSWER: Most existing manuscripts of the Bible are divided into two "families". These families are generally represented by the cities of Alexandria,Egypt and Antioch, Syria.

EXPLANATION: There are only two Bibles,God's and the devil's. There are only two views of the Bible. It is totally perfect or it is imperfect.

The two Bibles, in manuscript form, and their corresponding ideologies originate in two vastly different locations in the Mid East. Alexandria, Egypt and Antioch, Syria. Discerning which location gives us the perfect Bible and the correct ideology and which gave us the devil's bible and incorrect ideology is one of the easiest tasks imaginable. This pursuit is made childishly easy due to one source, **the Bible**.

As we have stated so many times, yet shall again, we accept the Bible as our final authority in all matters of **faith** and **practice**. Therefore, all anyone need do is to explore the Bible and discover what **GOD** thinks of Alexandria, Egypt and what He thinks of Antioch, Syria.

When studying Scripture a fundamental rule that is followed is called "the law of first mention". This means that it is **generally** true that the context in which someone or something is first mentioned sets the Bible attitude for that person or place.

In our study of Alexandria and Antioch we find it impossible to ignore the Bible's attitude toward Egypt itself.

Egypt

(1) Egypt is first mentioned in Genesis 12:10-12.

10 *"And there was a famine in the land: and Abram went down into Egypt to sojourn there: for the famine was grievous in the land.*

11 *And it came to pass, when he was come near to enter into Egypt, that he said unto Sarai his wife, Behold now, I know that thou art a fair woman to look upon:*

12 *Therefore it shall come to pass, when the Egyptians shall see thee, that they shall say, This is his wife: and they will kill me, but they will save thee alive."*

In Genesis 12:1-3 we find Abraham is given what is known as the Abrahamic Covenant. Literally it is God's promise to deliver the world to Abraham and his seed as their own private possession.

In Genesis 12:10 Abraham goes down into Egypt to escape a famine in his homeland. In verse 12 we find Abraham's fear that the Egyptians might kill him and steal Sarai his wife. **NOT** exactly a positive context. We see then that the **first** mention of **Egypt is negative**.

(2) In Exodus 1:11-14 we find that the Jews were slaves in Egypt.

11 *"Therefore they did set over them taskmasters to afflict them with their burdens. And they built for Pharaoh treasure cities, Pithom and Raames.*

12 *But the more they afflicted them, the more they multiplied and grew. And they were grieved because of the children of Israel.*

13 *And the Egyptians made the children of Israel to serve with rigour:*

14 *And they made their lives bitter with hard bondage, in mortar, and in brick, and in all manner of service in the field: all their service, wherein they made them serve, was with rigour."*

In fact, Pharaoh decrees that all male Jewish babies are to be killed in verses 15 and 16.

15 *"And the king of Egypt spake to the Hebrew midwives,*

*of which the name of the one was Shiphrah, and the name of
the other Puah:*

*16 And he said, When ye do the office of a midwife to the
Hebrew women, and see them upon the stools; if it be a son,
then ye shall kill him: but if it be a daughter, then she shall
live.''*

Obviously a **negative** connotation.

(3) In Exodus chapter 20, after He had brought the children
out of Egypt,God, **with His own voice**, tells what He thinks
of Egypt in verse 2 where He describes it as a "house of
bondage" *"I am the LORD thy God, which have brought thee
out of the land of Egypt, out of the house of bondage.''*

Again, a **negative** comment and this one directly from
God's lips.

(4) In Deuteronomy 4:20 Moses refers to Egypt as "the
iron furnace."

*"But the LORD hath taken you, and brought you forth out
of the iron furnace, even out of Egypt, to be unto him a people
of inheritance, as ye are this day.''*

(5) In Deuteronomy 17:16 Israel is told that, in the future,
when they have a king he is not to carry on commercial trade
with Egypt.

*"But he shall not multiply horses to himself, nor cause the
people to return to Egypt, to the end that he should multiply
horses: forasmuch as the LORD hath said unto you, Ye shall
henceforth return no more that way.''*

(6) And finally in Revelation 11:8, when God wants to
denounce Jerusalem, He compares it to Sodom and Egypt.

*"And their dead bodies shall lie in the street of the great
city, which spiritually is called Sodom and Egypt, where also
our Lord was crucified.''*

This brief study has shown what most Christians already
know. The Bible has a **negative** outlook on Egypt.

Alexandria

We find that Alexandria is mentioned only four times in
Scripture and that each mention is bad.

(1) Alexandria is **first mentioned** in Acts 6:9.

"Then there arose certain of the synagogue, which is

called the synagogue of the Libertines, and Cyrenians, and Alexandrians, and of them of Cilicia and of Asia, disputing with Stephen."

It was Jews from Alexandria who were in the crowd that disputed with and eventually killed Stephen.

(2) The second mention of Alexandria is in Acts 18:24.

"And a certain Jew named Apollos, born at Alexandria, an eloquent man, and mighty in the scriptures, came to Ephesus."

Here we find a Jew from Alexandria named Apollos who though fervent in spirit was misinformed concerning the gospel. Not knowing the true gospel of Jesus Christ he preached, in Ephesus, the baptism of John the Baptist. (Acts 18:25,19:3) Apollos was not saved and neither were his converts.

Later, Apollos is led to Christ by Aquila and Priscilla (verse 26) and gets his message straightened out (verse 28).

But in its second mention, Alexandria is synonymous with bad Bible teaching.

(3) The third and fourth mentions of Alexandria are very similar. After Paul is arrested in Acts 21 and appeals his case to Caesar he is sent to Rome, and eventual death, on a ship from, of all places Alexandria (Acts 27:6).

"And there the centurion found a ship of Alexandria sailing into Italy; and he put us therein."

(4) While sailing to Rome, Paul's ship is sunk in a tempest. After spending three months on the island of Melita he is sent on his way to eventual death on another ship. And where is this second ship from that is so ready to carry Paul to his death?

Acts 28:11: *"And after three months we departed in a ship of Alexandria, which had wintered in the isle, whose sign was Castor and Pollux."*

We see then that all four Bible references to Alexandria are negative. No one with any honesty could pretend that the Bible's representation of Alexandria is good.

It must also be noted here that Alexandria was a center of education and philosophy (Colossians 2:8) which it received from Athens in about 100 B.C. (Acts 17:16) There was a school of the Scriptures founded there by one Pantaenus who was a philosopher. Pantaenus interpreted scripture both philosophically and allegorically. That is to say that philosophically he believed truth to be relative, not absolute. He did not believe that the Bible was infallible. By looking at the Bible allegorically he believed that men such as Adam, Noah, Moses, and David existed only in Jewish poetry and were not true historical characters. He was succeeded as head of the school by Clement of Alexandria and later by Origen. Men who shared his skepticism.

It was Origen, deceived by the duel intoxicants of education and philosophy who upon receipt of pure copies of scripture altered them to parallel his twisted thinking. He is the father of all Bible critics and is not only responsible for the physical manuscripts which delete such verses as Luke 24:40, Acts 8:37 and I John 5:7, but he is also responsible for the Alexandrian philosophy parroted by so many of our fundamental scholars who claim that ''The Bible is perfect and infallible'' with one breath and then state ''The Bible has mistakes and mistranslations'' with the very next. It is this demented ideology that gave birth to the corrupt Alexandrian manuscripts in the first place. Thus we see that not only are the physical manuscripts of Alexandria corrupt and to be rejected, but the **Alexandrian philosophy**, that the Bible has mistakes in it and must be corrected, is even more subtle and dangerous and must be forsaken by **true** Bible believers.

Antioch

Ironically the **first mention** of Antioch is found in the very same book and chapter as Alexandria, Acts chapter 6, but in a radically different context.

(1) When the Apostles saw a need for helpers, helpers whom today we know as ''deacons'', they gave instructions for what kind of men should be chosen for the position.

Acts 6:3,4: *''Wherefore, brethren, look ye out among you seven men of honest report, full of the Holy Ghost and wisdom, whom we may appoint over this business.*

4 But we will give ourselves continually to prayer, and to the ministry of the word.''

The seven men chosen are listed in Acts 6:5.

QUESTION #8

"And the saying pleased the whole multitude: and they chose Stephen, a man full of faith and of the Holy Ghost, and Philip, and Prochorus, and Nicanor, and Timon, and Parmenas, and Nicolas a proselyte of Antioch:"

Please notice that one of the first deacons, Nicolas, was of Antioch. Is this a mere coincidence? Certainly not! Neither is it coincidental that Nicolas is the **only** deacon whose home town is given. Neither is it coincidental that Antioch is mentioned for the first time in Scripture in the same chapter in which Alexandria is mentioned. And it is certainly no difficult feat to see that one, Antioch, is first mentioned in a **positive** light and the other, Alexandria, is first mentioned in a negative light.

The next few pertinent appearances of Antioch start as a trickle and end as a flood of testimony to God's choice of Antioch for the center of His New Testament church.

(2) Antioch appears next in Scripture in Acts 11:19-21.

19 *"Now they which were scattered abroad upon the persecution that arose about Stephen traveled as far as Phenice, and Cyprus, and Antioch, preaching the word to none but unto the Jews only.*

20 *And some of them were men of Cyprus and Cyrene, which, when they were come to Antioch, spake unto the Grecians, preaching the Lord Jesus.*

21 *And the hand of the Lord was with them: and a great number believed, and turned unto the Lord."*

Here we find that certain of the Christians who had taken flight during the persecution preached the gospel as they fled.

Upon arrival in Antioch they, not knowing what had happened in Acts 10 with Peter opening the door of the gospel to the Gentiles, preached the gospel to the Grecians. Verse 21 tells us that God's Holy Spirit worked mightily in Antioch and that a "great number" were saved.

We see then that the first great Gentile awakening occurred in Antioch.

(3) In Acts 11:22-24 we find that Barnabus, (the son of consolation Acts 4:36) was sent to Antioch to see what was happening in Antioch.

22 *"Then tidings of these things came unto the ears of the*

church which was in Jerusalem: and they sent forth Barnabas, that he should go as far as Antioch.

23 Who, when he came, and had seen the grace of God, was glad, and exhorted them all, that with purpose of heart they would cleave unto the Lord.

24 For he was a good man, and full of the Holy Ghost and of faith: and much people was added unto the Lord."

Through the ministry of this great man of God, many more people were added to Christ.

(4) In Acts 11:25,26, two important facts are revealed.

25 "Then departed Barnabas to Tarsus, for to seek Saul: And when he had found him, he brought him unto Antioch.

26 And it came to pass, that a whole year they assembled themselves with the church, and taught much people. And the disciples were called Christians first in Antioch."

First, we find Barnabas departing for Tarsus to seek the young convert Saul. It was Barnabas who defended Paul's conversion to the doubting disciples in Acts 9: 26,27. Doubtless he was grieved to see the zealous young convert shipped off to Tarsus (Acts 9:30), and oblivion. Upon finding Saul, Barnabus does **not** bring him back to Jerusalem. (And certainly not to Alexandria.) He returns with him to Antioch, the spiritual capital of the New Testament church. All that Paul ever became,he owes to the gracious act of this godly old saint.

(5) In Acts 11:26 we find that born again believers were called "Christians" for the first time at Antioch. Thus every time we believers refer to ourselves as "Chrisitans" we complete a spiritual connection to our spiritual forefathers in Antioch. Antioch is to the Christian what Plymouth Rock is to the American.

(6) In verses 27 and 28 we find that God has now packed up His prophets and sent them north to Antioch.

27 "And in these days came prophets from Jerusalem unto Antioch.

28 And there stood up one of them named Agabus, and signified by the Spirit that there should be great dearth throughout all the world: which came to pass in the days of Claudius Caesar."

QUESTION #8

Jerusalem is left spiritually abandoned. Home only of the disciples, who were told to leave it years earlier in Acts 1:8.

(7) In Acts 11:29,30 we find that the saints ,**who God is blessing** in Antioch, must send monetary aid to the saints **who God is not blessing** in Jerusalem.

29 *"Then the disciples, every man according to his ability, determined to send relief unto the brethren which dwelt in Judaea:*

30 *Which also they did, and sent it to the elders by the hands of Barnabas and Saul."*

Yet these are not the final Biblical references to the capital of God's New Testament church.

(8) When God decides to send missionaries out into the world to preach the gospel, He never even glances in the direction of Jerusalem. (And most assuredly not Alexandria, Egypt) He looks instead to His faithful servants at Antioch.

Acts 13:1-3: *"Now there were in the church that was at Antioch certain prophets and teachers; as Barnabas, and Simeon that was called Niger, and Lucius of Cyrene, and Manaen, which had been brought up with Herod the tetrarch, and Saul.*

2 *As they ministered to the Lord, and fasted, the Holy Ghost said, Separate me Barnabas and Saul for the work whereunto I have called them.*

3 *And when they had fasted and prayed, and laid their hands on them, they sent them away."*

Thus, it is evident that the **first** missionary journey mentioned in Scripture originated in Antioch, with "Christians" from Antioch. And when this great work was fulfilled, no one wasted any time sightseeing or sending reports to Jerusalem. They simply returned to Antioch.

Acts 14:25-28: *"And when they had preached the word in Perga, they went down unto Attalia:*

26 *And thence sailed to Antioch, from whence they had been recommended to the grace of God for the work which they fulfilled.*

27 *And when they were come, and had gathered the church together, they rehearsed all that God had done with them, and how he had opened the door of faith unto the Gentiles.*

42

28 *And there they abode long time with the disciples.''*

Our last two glimpses of Antioch give evidence that to be in Antioch is to be in the middle of the will of God.

(9) In Acts chapter 15 the disciples in Jerusalem feel a need to send a pair of envoys to Antioch with their decrees concerning Gentile believers.

Acts 15:23-27: *"And they wrote letters by them after this manner; The apostles and elders and brethren send greeting unto the brethren which are of the Gentiles in Antioch and Syria and Cilicia:*

24 Forasmuch as we have heard, that certain which went out from us have troubled you with words, subverting your souls, saying, Ye must be circumcised, and keep the law: to whom we gave no such commandment:

25 It seemed good unto us, being assembled with one accord, to send chosen men unto you with our beloved Barnabas and Paul,

26 Men that have hazarded their lives for the name of our Lord Jesus Christ.

27 We have sent therefore Judas and Silas,who shall also tell you the same things by mouth.''

Following the completion of the mission, Judas returns to Jerusalem, **and oblivion**. Silas elects to stay in Antioch, and it is Silas who we find gaining a prominent place in Scripture as Paul's missionary partner on his second missionary journey.

(10) Of course, the second missionary journey did not originate in Jerusalem. It originated in the only place that it possibly could have, Antioch, as Acts 15:40 illustrates.

What was it about Antioch that was so attractive to God that He chose it as the center of New Testament Christianity?

It might be noted that, Antioch although it was a cultural center, had not abandoned itself to pagan religion, pagan education and pagan philosophy as had such prominent sites as Rome, Athens, and Alexandria.

It might also be weighed that Antioch, unlike the above mentioned cities, or even Jerusalem, was located almost exactly in the middle of the known world, and was built at the crossing of the East-West trade routes. It even boasted a sea port, via the Orontes River. These are all important attributes for the capital of Christianity, which is known for it's mobility.

It may be that many of the original autographs of Paul's epistles were penned in Antioch.

In the second century, a disciple by the name of Lucian founded a school of the Scriptures in Antioch. Lucian was noted for his mistrust of pagan philosophy. His school magnified the authority and divinity of Scripture and taught that the Bible was to be taken literally, not figuratively as the philosophers of Alexandria taught.

So Antioch is not only the point of origin for the correct family of Bible manuscripts, but is also the source for the ideology that accepts the Bible as **literally** and **perfectly** God's words. Today many well meaning, but "Alexandrian" educated preachers are uplifting the Antiochian Bible (King James) but with the Alexandrian conviction that it cannot be perfect. In fact, this Egyptian conviction states that there cannot be a perfect Bible on earth, in spite of God's promise in Psalm 12:6,7.

To accept the proper Book with an improper attitude will only predestine one to make the same mistakes and corruptions that their Egyptian fore fathers did.

Can **anyone** ignore a Bible admonition and not fall?

Solomon, the wisest man who ever lived, ignored the Biblical admonition to avoid Egypt and **not** go down to Egypt to multiply horses (Deuteronomy 17:16). In I Kings 3:1 he married Pharaoh's daughter. In I Kings 10:28 he had horses brought up out of Egypt. What was the result? By I Kings 11:3,4 we find that his heart had been turned away from following God. In verses 5-8 he began worshipping other gods. And by verses 9-43 God has pronounced judgment on him. If God doesn't want His people to go down to Egypt for horses, do we **dare** go there for a Bible or an ideology?

Solomon could not get away with ignoring the Bible's view of Egypt. Are **you** wiser than Solomon?

Question #9

QUESTION: What is the LXX?

ANSWER: A figment of someone's imagination.

EXPLANATION: First, let's define what the LXX is **supposed** to be. An ancient document called "The Letter of Aristeas" revealed a plan to make an **OFFICIAL** translation of the Hebrew Bible (the Old Testament) in Greek. This translation was to be accepted as the official Bible of the Jews and was to **replace** the Hebrew Bible. Supposedly this translation work would be performed by 72 Jewish scholars (?), six from each of the twelve tribes of Israel. The supposed location of the work was to be Alexandria, Egypt. The alleged date of translation was supposedly around 250 BC, during the 400 years of silence between the close of the Old Testament in 397 BC and the birth of Christ in approximately 4 BC (due to a four year error in the calendar).

It has become known as the Septuagint, "The Interpretation of the 70 Elders". Also it is represented by the Roman (?) numerals whose combined value is 70, hence L-50, X-10, X-10. Why it isn't called the *LXXII* I'll never know.

This so called "Letter of Aristeas" is the **sole** evidence for the existence of this mystical document. There are absolutely **NO** Greek Old Testament manuscripts existent with a date of 250 BC or anywhere near it. Neither is there any record in Jewish history of such a work being contemplated or performed.

When pressed to **produce** hard evidence of the existence of such a document, scholars quickly point to Origen's Hexapla written around 200 **AD**, or approximately 450 years later than the LXX was supposedly penned, and more than 100 years after the New Testament was completed. The second column of Origen's Hexapla contains **his own** (hardly 72 Jewish scholars) Greek translation of the Old Testament including spurious books such as ''Bel and the Dragon'', ''Judith'' and ''Tobit'' and other apocryphal books accepted as authoritative only by the Roman Catholic Church.

Proponents of the invisible LXX will try to claim that Origen didn't translate the Hebrew into Greek, but only copied the LXX into the second column of his Hexapla. Can this argument be correct? No. If it were, then that would mean that those astute 72 Jewish scholars added the Apocryphal books to their work **before they were ever written. (!)** Or else, Origen took the liberty to add these spurious writings to God's Holy Word (Rev. 22:18).

Thus we see that the second column of the Hexapla is Origen's personal, unveilable translation of the Old Testament into Greek and nothing more.

Eucebius and Philo, both of questionable character, make mention of a Greek Pentateuch. Hardly the entire Old Testament and not mentioned as any kind of an officially accepted translation.

Is there ANY Greek manuscript of the Old Testament written BEFORE the time of Christ? Yes. There is one minute scrap dated at 150 BC, the Ryland's Papyrus, #458. It contains Deuteronomy chapters 23-28. No more. No less. If fact, it may be the existence of this fragment that led Eucebius and Philo to **assume** that the entire Pentateuch had been translated by some scribe in an effort to interest Gentiles in the history of the Jews. It most certainly cannot be a portion of any pretended official Old Testament translation into Greek. We can rest assured that those 72 Jewish scholars supposedly chosen for the work in 250 BC would be just a mite feeble by 150 BC.

Besides the non-existence of any reason to believe such a translation was ever produced are several hurtles which the ''Letter of Ariteas'', Origen's Hexapla, Ryland's #458, and

Eucebius and Philo just **cannot clear**.

The first one is the "Letter of Aristeas" itself. There is little doubt amongst scholars today that it was **not** written by anyone named Ariteas. In fact, some believe its **true** author is Philo. This would give it an A.D. date. If this were true, then its **REAL** intention would be to deceive believers into thinking that Origen's second column is a copy of the LXX. A feat that it has apparently accomplished "in spades".

If there **was** an Aristeas, he was faced with two insurmountable problems.

First, how did he **ever** locate the twelve tribes in order to pick his six representative scholars from each. Having been thoroughly scattered by their many defeats and captivities, the tribal lines of the 12 tribes had long since dissolved into virtual non-existence. It was **impossible** for **anyone** to distinctly identify the 12 individual tribes.

Secondly, if the 12 tribes **had** been identified, they would not have undertaken such a translation for two compelling reasons.

(1) Every Jew knew that the official caretaker of Scripture was the tribe of Levi as evidenced in Deuteronomy 17:18, 31:25,26 and Malachi 2:7. Thus, **NO** Jew of any of the eleven other tribes would **dare** join such a forbidden enterprise.

(2) It is obvious to **any** reader of the Bible that the Jews were to be distinctly different from the Gentile nations around them. Unto them was given such distinct practices as circumcision, Sabbath worship, sundry laws of cleansing and their own homeland. Added to this is the heritage of the Hebrew language. Even today, practicing Jews in China and India refuse to teach their children any language but Hebrew. The Falasha Jews of Ethiopia were distinct among the many tribes of their country by the fact that they jealously retained the Hebrew language as an evidence of their Jewish heritage.

Are we to be so naive as to believe that the Jews who considered Gentiles nothing more than **dogs**, would willingly forsake their heritage, the Hebrew language, for a Gentile language into which would be translated the holiest possession of all, their Bible? Such a supposition is as insane as it is absurd.

"What then," one might ask, "of the numerous quotes in the New Testament of the Old Testament that are ascribed to the LXX?" The LXX they speak of is nothing more than the second column of Origen's Hexapla. The New Testament quotations are not quotes of any LXX **or** the Hexapla. They are the author, the Holy Spirit, taking the liberty of quoting His work in the Old Testament in whatever manner He wishes. And we can rest assured that He certainly is not quoting any non-existent Septuagint.

Only one more question arises. Then **why** are scholars so quick to accept the existence of this LXX in the face of such irrefutable arguments against it? The answer is sad and simple.

Hebrew is an extremely difficult language to learn. It takes years of study to attain a passing knowledge of it. And many more to be well enough versed to use it as a vehicle of study. By comparison a working knowledge of Greek is easily attainable. Thus, IF THERE WAS an official translation of the Old Testament into Greek, Bible critics could **triple** the field of influence overnight without a painstaking study of biblical Hebrew. Unfortunately, the acceptance of the existence of the Septuagint on such thin evidence is based solely on pride and voracity.

But stop and think. Even if such a spurious document as the LXX really did exist, how could a Bible critic, who, in reference to the King James Bible, say that "No translation has the authority of the original language," claim in the same breath that his pet LXX has equal authority with the Hebrew Original? This scholarly double-talk is nothing more than a self exalting authority striving to keep his scholarly position above those "unschooled in the original languages."

If you accept such an argument, I have a bridge to sell you in Brooklyn!

Question #10

QUESTION: What does this statement mean? "The King James Bible was good enough for the Apostle Paul, so it's good enough for me."

ANSWER: This statement is usually made in a sarcastic manner in order to embarrass Bible believers in their belief. The **FACT** is, the King James Bible **WAS** good enough for Paul. (See Question #11) But for now I'd like you to see that it was the only Bible that **Luke** would use.

EXPLANATION: In Acts 1:1,2 Luke makes the following statement: *"The former treatise have I made, O Theophilus, of all that Jesus began both to do and teach,*
Until the day in which he was taken up, after that he through the Holy Ghost had given commandments unto the apostles whom he had chosen:"
"The former treatise" is of course the Gospel of Luke which Luke wrote to a believer named Theophilus. Theophilus was apparently an early Christian who had never personally met the Lord while He was on this earth. Considering, though, that he was the recipient of both the Gospel of Luke and the Acts of the Apostles, he was most certainly one of the best informed.
Luke, in what may have been a passing comment, in the second verse of Acts chapter one, rings the death blow to the famous Nestle's Greek New Testament and also the New American Standard Version. Luke states that his "former treatise" told of all that Jesus began to do, and continued,

"until the day in which he was taken up." The things which Jesus began to do are first recorded in Luke 2:41-52 in which He was left behind in Jerusalem when Joseph and His mother left to return to Nazareth. This correlates with Acts 1:1. Luke's gospel is the only one of the four gospels which records any of Christ's actions prior to His baptism at the age of thirty years old. (Matthew 3:16, Mark 1:9 and John 1:29-34)

Luke's gospel ends with Christ being "carried up into heaven" in Luke 24:51. This correlates with Acts 1:2 "Until the day in which he was taken up."

Thus, Luke states that his gospel begins with the earliest acts of Christ and ends with His ascension. Therefore, any Greek manuscript or manuscripts, no matter what their age, containing the Gospel of Luke which omits either of these accounts is **not** authentic. In an examination of the 23rd Edition of Nestle's Greek Text we find that the Greek words, "Kai anepheroto eis ton huranon," "and was carried up into the heaven" are **not** found in this text.

The footnote in the critical apparatus indicates that the authority for removing this phrase is no more than manuscript (MS) Sinaiticus, D, one majuscule MS known as number 52 and **one** 5th century palimpsect (a MS which has been erased and written over top of). The phrase "and carried up into heaven" is found **in** B, C, E, F, G, H, L, S, T, V, Y, Z, Delta, Theta, Psi, and Omega plus papyrus p75, and most remaining witnesses. Yet on the basis of only two MSS the conservative scholars of the secret Lockman Foundation have omitted this phrase from Luke 24:51 in the New American Standard Version (NASV). Hence, the NASV is not truly a reliable translation. In fact, of most modern versions, only the "liberal" scholars of the Revised Standard Version (RSV) agreed with the "conservative" scholars of the NASV in omitting the phrase. Thus the known Communistic liberals of the RSV and the conservatives of the NASV are in full agreement that Christ did not asce nd bodily into heaven.

So we see that if Luke, the writer of the Gospel of Luke and the book of the Acts of the Apostles, could examine a King James Bible and a New American Standard Version he would declare the New American Standard Version a fraud and promptly proclaim the King James Bible as authentic.

Well, quite frankly, if it's good enough for **Luke**, it's good enough for **me**.

Question #11

QUESTION: I've heard that the italicized words in the King James Bible should be removed because they were added by the translators. Should they be removed?

ANSWER: If we remove **any** of the italicized words we must either remove them ALL or accept them ALL as Scripture.

EXPLANATION: Following are the problems with removing the italicized words from the Bible:

1. Anyone who has ever translated from one language to another knows that words **MUST** be added to the finished work to complete the sentence structure of the new language.

All translators do this when translating the Bible. The King James translators were men of integrity so they put the added words in italics.

Example #1

Psalm 23:1 reads "The LORD *is* my shepherd" in the King James Bible. The word "is" was added by the translators to complete the sense of the sentence.

Psalm 23:1 in the New International Version reads, "The LORD **is** my Shepherd."

So it is plain to see that **both** sets of translators added the same word to complete the sentence. Yet the King James translators put the word in italics to inform the reader that they had added it.

Example #2:

John 1:8 reads, "He was not that Light, but *was sent* to bear witness of that Light'' in the King James Bible.

John 1:8 reads, ''He was not that Light, but **was sent** to bear witness of that Light'' in the New King James Version.

Again **both** sets of translators have added words to their translation so that it would make sense. In this case it is the phrase ''was sent.'' Yet again, it is the King James translators who put their addition in italics for clarity.

Thus we see that the translators of our Bible should be commended on their integrity and ethics for their addition of the italicized words instead of castigated for a practice which **all** of our modern ''would be'' scholars follow routinely.

2. Critics of the Bible, fundamental or otherwise, claim that the italics can be removed, but NEVER remove them all. Usually they are stumped by a passage such as the word ''unknown'' in I Corinthians 14. Since they cannot explain the passage **with** the italicized word **in** the passage they make the thoughtless statement reproduced above and remove the problem word.

But this opens a tremendously large ''can of worms''! For if we say that italicized words do not belong in the text, we cannot say that **one** italicized word should be removed from the Bible, but we must say that **ALL** italicized words must be removed from the Bible. Even the casual student of Scripture knows that the Bible will make no sense at all if **ALL** italicized words are removed.

To remove **one** italicized word and leave another in is to claim **Divine Inspiration** in knowing which words should go and which words should stay.

Regardless of how great a preacher, soul-winner, or scholar might be none of us are going to bow our knees to them with the claim that they are **Divinely inspired** to reject or accept words in the Bible. If we are so foolish as to exalt a man's opinion in such a way, who should we exalt? There are hundreds of Bible critics who would vie for the office of ''Official Divinely Inspired Bible Corrector''. Who would be the lucky person? How would we choose him? And **WHO** would be so naive as to think that all Christians would follow his decrees? Yet **without** his decrees we have **NO WAY OF KNOWING** which italicized words belong in the Bible and which ones do not.

So we see that overcoming problem passages will require prayer and Bible reading instead of carelessly removing a troublesome word.

3. One of the classic defenses for leaving the italicized words alone is found in II Samuel 21:19.

"And there was again a battle in Gob with the Philistines, where Elhanan the son of Jaaroregim, a Bethlehemite, slew *the brother of* Goliath the Gittite, the staff of whose spear was like a weaver's beam."

By omitting the italicized words we have the Bible saying that **Elhanan** killed Goliath. Of course everyone knows that I Samuel 17 says that David killed Goliath. So we finally have the Bible that all lost men love to refer to when they say, "The Bible has contradictions in it".

Of course, our "Divinely Inspired Bible Corrector" would probably say the italics in II Samuel 21:19 do not need to be removed. But then who's to know **which** words to remove or which ones to keep in unless God "appeared" to them and told them.

4. Our fourth and best reason for not meddling with God's choice of words for His Bible comes from none other than the Apostles Peter and Paul and the Lord Jesus Christ Himself.

First, take a Bible (King James, of course) and read Psalm 16:8. I have set the LORD always before me: because *he is* at my right hand, I shall not be moved.

You will notice that the two words "he is" are in italics. Yet when we find the Apostle Peter quoting this verse in the New Testament in Acts 2:25 we find it says:

"For David speaketh concerning him, I foresaw the Lord always before my face, for he is on my right hand, that I should not be moved:"

So here we find the Apostle Peter quoting Psalm 16:8 **italicized words and all!** You would almost believe that God wanted them in there wouldn't you?

Now it might be pointed out that Peter was an unlearned and ignorant man (Acts 4:13) and so, lacking the "benefits" of a Bible college education, he blindly accepted the Bible (King James?) as every word of God. But let us look at the same phenomena concerning the Apostle Paul and the Lord Jesus Christ.

Paul, as did other New Testament writers, often quoted from the Old Testament in his writings. In doing so, he quoted as did the others directly from the Hebrew Text. We have several of Paul's quotes which contain words not found in the Hebrew original.

In Romans 10:20 Paul quotes Isaiah 65:1.

Romans 10:20: "But Esaias is very bold, and saith, I was found of them that sought me not; I was made manifest unto them that asked not after me."

Isaiah 65:1: "I am sought of them that asked not for me; I am found of *them that* sought me not: I said, Behold me, behold me, unto a nation that was not called by my name."

Yet we see that the words "them that" which Paul quoted as though they were **in** Isaiah 65:1 exist only in the italics of the King James Bible.

The same is true of I Corinthians 3:20, "And again, The Lord knoweth the thoughts of the wise, that they are vain." which is a quote of Psalm 94:11, "The LORD knoweth the thoughts of man, that they *are* vanity." where we find the word "are" supplied by the translators.

But the most unexplainable is Paul's quote of Deuteronomy 25:4 in I Corinthians 9:9. For it is written in the law of Moses, Thou shalt not muzzle the mouth of the ox that treadeth out the corn. Doth God take care for oxen?

Deut 25:4: "Thou shalt not muzzle the ox when he treadeth out *the corn*."

Here we find Paul quoting the words "the corn" just as if they had been in the Hebrew original even though they are only found in the italics of our Authorized Version!

If one were to argue that Paul was quoting a supposed Greek Septuagint translation of the original Hebrew, our dilemma only worsens. For now, two perplexing questions present themselves to us. First, if such a Greek translation ever existed, (which is not documented in history) by what authority did the translators insert these words? Secondly, if they were added by the translators, does Paul's quoting of them confirm them as inspired?

While you ponder these important questions, we will note that **Jesus** also quoted from what appears to have been a King James Bible.

We find Him quoting a word that wasn't in the "originals". In fact, a word that only exists in the italics found in the pages of the King James Bible.

Read below, please, Deuteronomy 8:3.

"And he humbled thee, and suffered thee to hunger, and fed thee with manna, which thou knewest not, neither did thy fathers know; that he might make thee know that man doth not live by bread only, but by every *word* that proceedeth out of the mouth of the LORD doth man live."

You will note that the word "word" is in italics, meaning of course, that it was not in the Hebrew text. Upon examination of Deuteronomy 8:3 in Hebrew one will find that the word "dabar" which is Hebrew for "word" is not found anywhere in the verse.

Yet in His contest with Satan we find Jesus quoting Deuteronomy 8:3 as follows in Matthew 4:4.

"But he answered and said, It is written, Man shall not live by bread alone, but by every word that proceedeth out of the mouth of God."

While quoting Deuteronomy 8:3 Jesus quotes the entire verse **including the King James italicized word!** Even an amateur "scholar" can locate "ramati", a form of "rama", which is Greek for "word", in any Greek New Testament.

So, just as critics of the Bible like to joke and say, "Well, the King James was good enough for the Apostle Paul so it's good enough for me." A true Bible-believer can truly say, "Well, the King James was good enough for the Apostles Peter and Paul and for the Lord Jesus Christ, so it's good enough for me".

So we see we have three options on what to do with the italicized words in the Bible.

(1) Remove **All** of them.

(2) Exalt one of our fundamental Bible critics to the office of "Official Divinely Inspired Bible Corrector" and then give his decrees all the weight and allegiance that we would give to Jesus Christ.

(3) Leave **all** the words in our divinely inspired Bible alone, and trust that just **maybe** Jesus Christ is correct.

It's as though we **had** a choice.

Question #12

QUESTION: Aren't there some great men who use other versions?

ANSWER: Yes, but they are all in subjection to the perfect Bible.

EXPLANATION: There are preachers who are considered "great" by many who either openly or covertly disdain the concept of the Bible being perfect. They correct it with regularity and openly attack those who claim to accept it as infallible.

There are also many Christian colleges and universities where a student is shown "mistakes" in the King James Bible. The obvious question is: "How can these great men and institutions be wrong and still have God bless them"? The answer is found in the Bible, our final authority in all matters of **faith** and **practice**.

As we turn to II Kings 17 we find Israel in a sad state. They have been conquered by Assyria and the Israelites were carried away captive, II Kings 17:23. The king of Assyria then planted heathen foreigners in the land of Israel, II Kings 17:24. These people did not fear God so He sent lions among them to kill them, verse 25, causing them to cry out for Jewish priests to be sent to teach them how to worship "the God of the land", II Kings 17:26-28. The result is found in verses 32 and 41. The Bible says that, "They feared the LORD, **and** served their own gods".

This same thing is true among our fundamental preachers

and colleges. Many fundamental preachers really do not believe that the Bible is infallible, but they dare not admit it. So they "fear the LORD," ie, they stand in the pulpit, hold the Bible in the air and declare, "This Book is the absolute word of God without a mixture of error". Then, out of the pulpit they "serve their own gods" in that they privately point to what they consider mistakes in the Bible and ridicule anyone who **really believes what they had just said in the pulpit**. This may seem hypocritical. It is. It may seem two-faced. It is. But rest assured, they would never **say** that they believe the Bible is perfect while standing in the pulpit if they didn't "Fear the LORD" enough to know that they would be ruined if anyone knew what they **really** believed. In other words, you'll never hear one of them stand in the pulpit, hold up the Bible and say, "I believe that this Book is poorly translated and full of errors and that **there isn't a perfect version on the face of this earth that you can hold in your hand**". If they ever made such an honest confession they know that they would be "through". Thus God's "lions" **MAKE** them bow their knees to the perfect Bible **even** if they do it only as lip service.

Likewise, our Christian colleges and universities dare not say, "Come to our school and we will destroy your faith in the perfect Bible and show you that it is filled with errors". No, to only "serve their own gods" in such a way would bring the "lions" to the campus doors. They "Fear the LORD" enough to advertise themselves as schools who "Stand without apology for the absolute authority of Scripture" or some even go so far as to boast "We use only the King James Bible". Then, **after** the student has been accepted, **after** the student has committed himself to the school, then and only then, do they begin ever so subtly to **destroy their faith in the perfect Bible and show that the "good old King James" is full of errors**. But they know, and God knows that they were too scared not to bend their knees to "the God of the land" and His Book, the King James Bible.

Question #13

QUESTION: Where was the Bible before 1611?

ANSWER: In the available Antiochian manuscripts.

EXPLANATION: Critics of the perfect Bible like to throw out this question as though it will ''stun'' Bible believers. It doesn't.

The overwhelming majority of Bible manuscripts existent throughout history have been the text found in Antioch. They have always been available in some form, either in copies of the original Greek, or the old Latin of 150 AD, (**NOT** to be confused with Jerome's corrupt ''Vulgate'') or the Syrian Peshetto of 157 AD.

That it would be difficult indeed to gather all of these sources together and place them in the hands of the common man gives credence to God's reasoning for the collation and translation of the King James Bible.

Question #14

QUESTION: Did the translators of the Authorized Version claim to be inspired by God?

ANSWER: No. But Biblically that does not mean that they could not have been inspired.

EXPLANATION: The men on the translation committee of the King James Bible were, without dispute, the most learned men of their day and vastly qualified for the job which they undertook. They were overall both academically qualified by their cumulative knowledge and spiritually qualified by their exemplary lives.

Among their company were men who, academically, took a month's vacation and used the time to learn and master an entirely foreign language; wrote a Persian dictionary; invented a specialized mathematical ruler; one was an architect; mastered oriental languages; publicly debated in Greek; tutored Queen Elizabeth in Greek and mathematics; and of one it was said,"Hebrew he had at his fingers end". Yet **head** knowledge can be a curse if not tempered by a fervent, pious heart.

In this, the spiritual realm, they were light years ahead of many today who flaunt their education yet fail in any attempt at a practical, personal witness.

This company was blessed with men known for their zeal and tact in debating and converting Romanists to Christ. They spent hours in private and family devotions. Many did the work of evangelism and even that of missionary representatives of later Queen Elizabeth. One, lived to the age of one hundred and three years. In the closing years of his life, after preaching for two full hours he said to his congregation, "I will no longer trespass on your patience" to which the entire congregation cried out with one consent, "For God's sake go on". He then continued his exposition of the Word of God at length.

Yet humanity was a universal trait shared among them as is so amply revealed in the Epistle Dedicatory.

"So that if, on the one side, we shall be traduced by Popish Persons at home or abroad, who therefore will malign us, because we are poor instruments to make God's holy Truth to be yet more and more known unto the people, whom they desire still to keep in ignorance and darkness; or if, on the other side, we shall be maligned by selfconceited Brethren, who run their own ways, and give liking unto nothing, but what is framed by themselves, and hammered on their anvil;"

Yet, in spite of their outstanding character, they never claimed divine inspiration. (A claim which, if they **had** made, would overjoy their detractors as evidence of a prideful spirit.) They never even claimed perfection for their finished work.

Does this mean that, because they did not **claim** God's hand in translating the Scripture that He could not be or was not in control of their commission? For the answer we must look to the Bible, our final authority in all matters of **faith** and **practice**.

When John the Baptist was accosted by the Levites in John chapter one, and asked if he was Elijah (John 1:21) he answered that he was **not** Elijah. Yet in Matthew chapters 11:7-14 and 17:10-13 Jesus Christ plainly stated that John was Elijah.

Did John the Baptist lie? No. Did Jesus Christ lie? Of course not. The answer is very simply that John **was** Elijah **but he didn't know it!** Thus we see from our **Bible example** that a man can have God working through him and not know it. Likewise, God could easily have divinely directed the King James translators without their active knowledge.

Question #15

QUESTION: Aren't today's scholars better equipped totranslate the Bible than the King James translators were?

ANSWER: No.

EXPLANATION: The answer to the question is ''No'' for two reasons.

First is that, the scholarship of the men who translated the King James Bible is literally unsurpassable by today's scholars. Two books available best illustrate this and should be read by anyone who wants to seriously study the subject. They are <u>Translators</u> <u>Revived</u>, by Alexander McClure, Maranatha Publications, and <u>The</u> <u>Men</u> <u>Behind</u> <u>the</u> <u>King</u> <u>James</u> <u>Version</u>, by Gustavus Paine, Baker Book House.

The men of the King James translation committee were scholars of unparalleled ability. A brief description of their several abilities is found under a previous section.

Secondly, it would be foolish and contradictory to believe that today's scholars **ever could** equal or surpassthose of the Authorized Version.

Most Christians agree that the world, with time, degenerates. Morals have degenerated since 1611. Character has degenerated since 1611. Even our atmosphere has degenerated. Are we then to believe that education has gotten better? Only a worshiper of education could pretendto believe such a fairytale. Education has degenerated along with the entire world system and could never produce a scholar equal to those of nearly four hundred years ago.

Question #16

QUESTION: Did King James authorize his translation to beused in the churches in England?

ANSWER: No. He authorized it's translation, but not itsusage.

EXPLANATION: It is difficult for someone in the twentiethcentury, especially someone in America to fathom the conditions of nearly four hundred years ago. We Christians not only have a Bible in our language, but more often than not, we have several. Added to that is our concordance and a raft of Bible commentaries and sundry other "Christian" books.

Yet the world of the sixteenth and early seventeenth centuries was quite different. The common man in England had no Bible. The only copy available to him was chained to the altar of the church. As recently as 1536, William Tyndale had been burned at the stake for the high crime of printing Bibles in the language of the common man, English. When King James commissioned the fifty-four translators in 1603 he did not mandate the upcoming translation to be used in churches. In fact, that it was translated and **not** intended for the churches left it only one explainable destiny. That is, that it should be supplied to the common man.

It might be noted that the world has no greater power than the common man with the common Bible in his hand.

Question #17

QUESTION: If King James didn't authorize the Bible for use in churches, who was it translated for?

ANSWER: The common man.

EXPLANATION: There is so much made of the perfection, or supposed imperfection, of the Bible that one element in the equation is often overlooked. That is, the reason for having a perfect Bible in the first place, the **common man**. If there was no common man, there would be no need for a Bible in the common language.

Let us remember that **the church** (any religious organization in this case) has **always** had access to scripture. The result of their having the Bible has generally tended toward pride and a sense of "lording" over the flock. But put the Bible in the hands of the common man and it is a different story. It has been said, "Put a beggar on horseback and he'll ride off at a gallop." This best describes a common man's reaction to being given a perfect Bible.

The common man is the moving (but not directing) force of the world. He is needed to fill everything from armies to churches. He is the consumer and not a gas station or grocery store can survive without him. He obediently serves the state with little interest or information concerning who is governing his life. His energy is used for profit by those in control of him, but he must never be given the power of government. He may be allowed to vote for those governing him, but he must be kept out of the governmental system himself.

The same is true in the ecclesiastical realm. Indeed, he **should** be in subjection to his pastor, but **no one** has the right to keep him ignorant of his Creator's will for his life. That will is found in the Bible.

Over the centuries, the prime violator in this area has been the Roman Catholic Church. The Roman Catholic Church has gone to great lengths to keep its people and others ignorant of the Scriptures. Roman Catholics are generally told that they can't understand the Bible. You can understand the chagrin of a Roman Catholic priest when one of his church members gets a Bible in his own language and claims to be able to understand it.

The war that the Roman Catholic Church has waged against the Bible has been carried out primarily in two ways.

1. Keep the people ignorant by controlling access to the Bible.

2. Counter God's Bible with one of their own.

Access to the Bible is controlled in two ways. First, the common man is persuaded that he cannot understand the Scripture and must subject himself to the authority of his priest and his private interpretation. Where this method can't be used, such as with non-Catholics, the Roman Catholic Church seeks to establish itself as a controlling factor in the government (preferably the state religion) and then physically confiscates all copies of the Bible and destroys them. Objectors are killed. This pattern has been followed by the Roman Catholic Church for centuries with great success.

The second method to eliminate the Bible is to replace it with one of Roman Catholic making. These then are used to fill any gap left by the confiscation of the true Bible.

In history this has been done several times. When the Roman Catholic Church saw the popularity and the threat of the Old Latin Bible (called the Vulgate from the Latin ''vulgar'' meaning ''common'') of 150 AD they had their **own** Latin Bible translated from manuscripts which had been corrupted in Alexandria, Egypt. This work was foisted upon a reluctant Roman Catholic scholar by the name of Jerome and upon publication in 380 AD was promptly and shamelessly entitled ''The Vulgate''. This worthless book sat unused for 800 years until the Roman Catholic Church "eliminated the competition" by burning all of the original (good) Vulgates **along with their owners**. This, of course, ushered in the Dark Ages, a time of unsurpassed power for the Roman Catholic Church. To this day,most people upon hearing acclaim for the Latin Vulgate (the good one, 150 AD) erroneously attribute it to the usurping Roman Catholic Vulgate of 380 AD.

Most new English translations available today are from these same corrupt Roman Catholic manuscripts. In the hands of the common man, these bibles do nothing. They are perfectly safe to "the powers that be".

King James, whether he knew it or not, gave the common man **back** his most valued possession, the true Bible inEnglish. (The Roman Catholic Church had translated its own English Bible in 1582 in Rheims, France. It was worthless.) King James and his translating committee may have never expected their new translation to go any farther than the shores of England. But God and the common man saw fit to carry it around the globe.

Today the common man is in grave danger of having his perfect Bible stolen from him again. This is being accomplished by two methods.

First, an attempt is being made (and has been underway for almost 100 years) to **physically** replace the King JamesBible with bibles translated from corrupt Roman Catholic manuscripts. These books are powerless and worthless, perfect for the job. Sadly, the King James Bible is being attacked by many saved, fundamental teachers and preachers who really may be well intentioned, but who do enjoy the feeling of authority (Roman Catholic, pope-like authority) and power that being able to "correct" the Bible brings them. This all important transition is taking place in both churches and Bible colleges. ("Bible-believing" Bible colleges at that.)

The second area of conquest is the very **brain** of the common man, and it also is carried out in two phases.

The first is the "suppressive phase" in which the victim is bombarded with so much anti-King James propaganda that he is spiritually suppressed from mentally accepting the true, perfect Bible. This method robs his **brain** of the Bible even though his **hand** may possess it. In other words, his Bible has been stolen from his brain but not taken from him physically. (Yet!)

The second phase is the "brain washing phase." This is carried out by preachers, teachers and especially the "Christian" media. Christian radio stations have almost universally desisted from using the King James Bible. They have "Bible readings", daily memory verses, and even read the Christmas story in Luke 2 from **any** bible but the King James. This robs the **subconscious** mind of the true Bible. For you see, many Bible rejecting preachers, upon trying to preach from a new version are confronted by some "unlearned and ignorant" (Acts 4:13) church member who, though unable to argue down the pastor's sales pitch concerning the new translation, retorts with, "But that just doesn't 'sound' like **the Bible.**"

By constantly hearing other versions read over radio, TV or in Christian schools the younger generation of Christians will never have the benefit of subconsciously **knowing** what **"The Bible"** sounds like.

So we see that the **real** enemy of the Roman Catholic Church and the Roman Catholic totalitarian spirit found among some fundamentalists is **NOT** just the Bible. **It is the Bible in the hand and heart of the common man.** The same person that the devil hates and hopes to fill Hell with.

Has **your** Bible been stolen from your hand? What about your **brain?**

Question #18

QUESTION: Someone said, "The King James Bible is the Word of God because I got saved through it!" Is that statement correct?

ANSWER: No.

EXPLANATION: The Bible is infallible and perfect without any influence by **any** sinner. By accepting Christ as our personal Saviour we impart nothing to Scripture, though God imparts eternal life to us.

Many have been led to Christ by someone using other versions. I once spoke with a man who vehemently claimed that the *Good News For Modern Man* was the infallible Word of God because someone had led **him** to Christ using it. Wrong! His getting saved through a *Good News For Modern Man* did not correct so much as **one** of the many gross inaccuracies in that version.

I have a friend who believes the Bible (KJV) to be the infallible, perfect Word of God. Yet he himself was led to Christ by someone using a *Living Bible*. Did the *Living Bible* become the infallible Word of God the moment he believed? Of course not. It never was perfect and never will be. But if it **did** become perfect because he got saved through it, would it not have **lost** its perfection when he chose to use the King James?

So we see that the Bible, King James of course, is the infallible, perfect Word and words of God regardless of what someone used to lead you or I to Christ. In fact, it would still be the perfect infallible Word and words of God, even if we hadn't gotten saved at all.

Question #19

QUESTION: Are people who believe the King James Bible "church splitters?"

ANSWER: No. The only church that a believer in the perfect Bible could possibly split would have to be one that **didn't** believe that the Bible was perfect.

EXPLANATION: Sometimes false accusations are based on misunderstandings. Sometimes they are based upon utter and complete falsehood. The fallacy that people believing in the perfect Bible are church splitters is unfortunately based entirely and maliciously on falsehood.

Sadly, there are **many** Christians who have been through the traumatizing experience of a church split. It would be erroneous to pretend that every church split was caused by someone believing that the King James Bible was perfect.

Churches split over everything from money issues to the question of what color to paint the new auditorium. The FACT of the matter is that Christians sadly lack the grace found in Romans 14 and Luke 17:1-5. It has nothing to do with the King James Bible. To try to claim that it does is to be a great deal less than honest.

Question #20

QUESTION: Aren't all King James Bible believers "name callers?"

ANSWER: No.

EXPLANATION: In recent years, the issue of a perfect Bible has been expertly handled by Dr. Peter S. Ruckman. Dr. Ruckman is a highly educated teacher/preacher who accepts the Antiochian manuscript as authentic and views them with the Antiochian ideology that accepts the Bible as perfect.

Dr. Ruckman's style is forceful in regard to the authority of Scripture and his treatment of Bible critics is devastating. His approach to most Bible issues is one of grace, where many Christians lack such grace. But on the singular issue of the authority of Scripture his approach is similar to the Apostle Paul (II Corinthians 10:10) and the great English scholar, John William Burgon.

A very few advocates of the perfect Bible, lacking Dr. Ruckman's scholastic qualifications have assimilated his caustic style with tragic results.

The broad majority of King James Bible believers do not utilize this style simply because it is not their natural style.

Question #21

QUESTION: Don't King James Bible believer's "worship" theBible? Didn't God destroy the originals because He didn't want these people to venerate them?

ANSWER: No and no.

EXPLANATION: Many critics of the perfect Bible have become very frustrated in recent years. This is due to the fact that their entire argument against the Bible has been systematically destroyed by historical fact, their own shortfall of scholastic ability and the consistent blessing of the King James Bible by the Holy Spirit.

In a desperate attempt to "sling mud" at Bible believers, they make the two statements found above.

Do King James Bible believers worship the Bible? No. They do not pray to it as they do to Jesus Christ. They do not preach that "the Bible saves" but that **Jesus** saves.They blissfully mark notes all over their Bibles, though none would dare to do so to Jesus Christ.

There is not even enough evidence to **mistakenly** believe that King James Bible believers worship the Bible. Therefore, the charge is unfortunately born of malice not sincerity.

Did God destroy the originals to keep King James Bible believers from someday worshipping them? No. Nothing could be farther from fact.

God allowed the originals to pass off the scene because their only value was their words, which He preserved through copies. Once the originals had served their purpose and were copied, they received no loyalty from God or His people.

If the originals were somehow to "miraculously" appear today, they would be of little interest to Bible believers since they make little of them now.

If anyone would venerate them, it would probably be the crowd that makes so much of them today, **the Bible critics.**

Question #22

QUESTION: Aren't King James Bible believers a cult?

ANSWER: No.

EXPLANATION: The charge that King James Bible believers are a cult is similar to the charge that they worship the Bible. It is a result of the same frustration and born of the same malice. Sadly, when facts do not prove them right, character assassination is in order.

Cults are somewhat difficult to define, although there are two outstanding characteristics evident in all cults.

First, a cult has a central body that makes decisions for all of its disciples. Most King James Bible believers are fiercely independent and many times disagree about other doctrines, even with one another. Their only central authority is the Bible, not a college or university.

Secondly, most cults fear that their disciples will investigate their opposition's beliefs and then be converted by the truth. Therefore they make strict rules disallowing books and materials that disagree with their doctrine.

Again, since the **facts** support the Authorized Version, King James Bible believers are not afraid to study the charges of their critics. In fact, this book attempts to confront all of the Bible critic's charges with complete candor.

Now, it will be noted that, there are some Bible colleges and universities which have a policy of confiscating books which support the view of a perfect Bible. In fact, **this** book may be on that list someday.

It makes one wonder just **who** is the "cult" and who isn't.

Question #23

QUESTION: Is it "heresy" to believe that the King James Bible is perfect?

ANSWER: No.

EXPLANATION: It is amusing yet appalling that a King James Bible believer, who **BELIEVES** the Bible to be inerrant, is called a "heretic" by people who **claim** to believe that the Bible is inerrant.

"Heresy", according to Webster, is "an opinion or doctrine contrary to the truth or to generally accepted beliefs."

It is "generally accepted" that the Bible is the perfect word of God. I have often told people, "I don't believe that the King James Bible is the inerrant word of God. I believe that the **BIBLE** is the inerrant word of God. But if you ask me to **give** you a copy of that Bible, I'll hand you a King James Bible."

Critics of the King James Bible **believe** that the "Bible" is the inerrant word of God. BUT, ask them to **hand you a copy** of that inerrant Bible that they "believe" in, and you will find that **it doesn't exist anywhere on this earth!**

We King James Bible believers simply believe what they CLAIM to believe. And for that we are called "heretics."

Actually the "heretic" label is designed more to scare young adherents away from the inerrant Bible, than to honestly define the name callers feelings. It is hoped by the Bible critic that the fear of being labeled a "heretic" will discourage zealous Christians from **REALLY** believing what Bible critics **claim** to believe.

In fact, if it is "generally accepted by fundamentalists that "the Bible is the inerrant word of God" and the Bible critic can find a mistake in **every** Bible that you put in his hand, then...who really is the heretic?

Question #24

QUESTION: Who was Dean Burgon?

ANSWER: He was an outstanding 19th century Bible scholar.

EXPLANATION: John William Burgon (1813-1888) was a man of tremendous intellect and ranks among men such a Lancelot Andrews (1555-1626) and Robert Dick Wilson (1856-1930) in scholarship. He became the Dean of Chichester and has since been known as "Dean" Burgon.

Dr. Burgon was contemporary with Westcott and Hort. He was an advocate of the Textus Receptus and was the nemesis of Westcott and Hort's feeble arguments against it. He believed, unlike Westcott and Hort, in basing all conclusions on the solid foundation of **facts** rather than the **sand** of theory. He would leave no stone unturned in his quest for truth and no blow undelivered in his defense of it.

His serious scholarship, quick wit and acid tongue drove Westcott and Hort and all other Alexandrian scholars from the field of battle. His arguments against the Alexandrian text and in favor of the last 12 verses of Mark and other questioned portions have proven to be as unanswerable by modern scholarship as they were to his contemporaries.

Today his name is as synonymous with the defense of the King James Bible as the names of Hills, Fuller and Ruckman. He is not only known as a champion of the Authorized Bible, but his works are an example of what **honest, objective** and **thorough** scholarship can produce.

Question #25

QUESTION: What is the difference between a "Textus Receptus Man" and a "King James Man?"

ANSWER: A "TR Man" gets his manuscripts from Antioch and his philosophy from Egypt.

EXPLANATION: Under Question #8 concerning Alexandria and Antioch it was pointed out that we derive two things from each of these locations. We derive **manuscripts** and an **ideology** through which we judge those manuscripts.

From Alexandria we receive corrupted manuscripts, tainted by the critical hand of Origen. We also receive an ideology that believes the Bible to be divine, but **not** perfect, not without error.

From Antioch we receive the pure line of manuscripts culminating in what is known as the "Received Text" or Textus Receptus. We also receive the ideology that the Bible is not only Divine, but perfect, without error.

1. **Most** Bible critics do not believe that the Bible is perfect (The Alexandrian Ideology). They usually also accept the Alexandrian manuscripts as superior to those of Antioch.

2. A King James Bible believer accepts the Antiochian manuscripts or Textus Receptus as superior to the Alexandrian. They also accept the Antiochian Ideology in that they accept the Bible as infallible and do not believe it contains any errors or mistranslations and that it **cannot be improved.**

3. A Textus Receptus man also accepts the Antiochian manuscripts or Textus Receptus as superior to the Alexan-

drian. But a Textus Receptus man accepts the Antiochian manuscripts yet he views them with the Alexandrian Ideology.

He does not accept any translation as perfect and without error. He generally feels that the King James is the **best** translation but can be improved. He usually stumbles at Acts 12:4 and states that it is a mistranslation.

This contradiction is **NOT** the result of a bad or dishonest heart so much as it is the result of a bad education. Most Textus Receptus men have been taught by others who have been deceived into accepting, **unconsciously,** the Alexandrian Ideology.

Question #26

QUESTION: Will a Bible college education clear up the controversy over the issue of a perfect Bible?

ANSWER: No. About ninety-nine out of one hundred times a Bible college education will either confuse or destroy a student's faith in the perfect Bible.

EXPLANATION: There are many benefits to a Bible college education. A student can learn invaluable lessons on pastoring and church planting. A student weak on doctrine can be grounded in his faith. Friendships and experiences from Bible college days will often last a life time.

Unfortunately, faith that God has a perfect Bible is more often than not a **victim** of Bible college education rather than a beneficiary. The reason is simple. Most Bible colleges are staffed by very well meaning men, many who do indeed love the Lord, who are victims of Alexandrian teaching.

Others, though set right about the proper manuscript family are still unconsciously afflicted with a faith in the Bible that is weakened by the Alexandrian Ideology. They cannot mentally accept the belief that the Bible, **the one in their hand,** is truly perfect.

Sometimes, even schools which advertise that they are "King James Only" or "Textus Receptus Only" are still afflicted with this malady. Thus, a student will find himself confused when he hears his Bible **corrected** in a college that claims to accept the Bible as perfect. Most often, he will succumb to the diatribe and also become a critic of the perfect

Bible. If he does not accept the school's position he will usually be branded as a "fanatic" and ostracized and sometimes even dismissed.

This does not mean that a Bible college education does not have its advantages. It **does** mean however that a Bible college education seldom strengthens a student's faith that the Bible is perfect.

Question #27

QUESTION: Do Christians and Preachers who use other bibles ''hate God?''

ANSWER: No, although some may abhor the thought of being in subjection to ''a Book.''

EXPLANATION: In Mark 9:38-41 we find the disciples upset with someone who did not ''follow'' them. Yet the Lord told them to leave the man alone.

God desires worship and love from His creatures. There are many Preachers who, as Bible college students were misled concerning the King James Bible. They may very well love Jesus Christ but through ignorance or deceit use the wrong bible. They certainly do **not** ''hate God''.

It has been found however that someone who loves the Lord and uses the wrong bible must one day face the Bible issue and make a choice between right and wrong. If they chose ''right'' their faith is strengthened and they will cease to use other bibles and usually cease to attempt to ''correct'' the Bible while reading or preaching.

Some however, upon reaching the point of decision, rebel at the thought that their ''Alma Mater'' could be wrong. They would sooner believe that the Bible is wrong. One preacher was heard to say, ''I accept the teaching that the King James Bible is perfect, but I can't **stand** for it because my 'Alma-Mater' doesn't take that stand.''

Sometimes they weigh the damage to their prestige amongst their peers and feel that they cannot afford to take a stand for

God's perfect Bible. One can imagine the financial damage a college professor might experience if he took an Antiochian stand in an Alexandrian school.

Unfortunately, you cannot serve God **and** mammon. Therefore, one who for whatever reason rejects the teaching that the Bible is perfect in English usually becomes antagonistic toward those who disagree with him. Usually, his contempt is generated more as a defensive measure than intellectual conviction. **But he dare not let you know this.**

It can happen that a Christian simply refuses to be in subjection to what he considers a mere book. He rejects the authority of Scripture **in his life.** It must be rememberedthat the Pharisees hated Jesus because He spoke as one with **authority** (Matthew 7:29) and **not** as the scholars of His day.

Question #28

QUESTION: Is the King James Bible inspired or preserved?

ANSWER: The original autographs were **inspired.** The King James Bible is those same autographs **preserved** up to today.

EXPLANATION: The best way to **simply** describe inspiration and preservation of the Bible is as follows:

Inspiration is when God takes a **blank** piece of paper (papyrus, vellum, etc.) and uses men to write His words.

Preservation is when God takes those words **already written** and uses men to preserve them to today.

Both of these actions are **DIVINE** and are assured by God as recorded in Psalm 12:6,7.

6 *"The words of the LORD are pure words: as silver tried in a furnace of earth, purified seven times.*

7 *Thou shalt keep them, O LORD, thou shalt preserve them from this generation for ever."*

In Psalm 12:6 God assures us that His originals are perfect. Even though penned by fallible men with the heinous sins of; murder (Moses and David), adultery (David), idolatry (Solomon), and denial of the Lord (Peter). God's words are untainted by the sins of the penmen.

That the originals were inspired perfect in their entirety is an undisputed belief among fundamentalists today.

But most fundamentalists argue that only the ''originals''were perfect. They say that today we have nothing but copies and translations of those copies. They seem indignant at the thought that any "mere translation" should be considered a perfect copy of the originals. They claim that copies and translations are products of uninspired men and therefore must all contain mistakes.

Fundamentalists clinging to this tenet are mislead. Their folly in accepting this erroneous teaching is fourfold.

1. It is somewhat confusing and unexplainable that a person could claim that God could not use, sinful men to **preserve** His words when **all** fundamentalists believe that he used sinful men to write His **inspired** words. Certainly a God who had enough power to **inspire** His words would alsohave enough power to preserve them. I highly doubt that He has **lost** such ability over the years.

2. Why would God inspire the originals and then lose them? Why give a **perfect** Bible to men like Peter, John, James, Andrew and company and not us? **They** had seen, heard, and touched the Lord (I John 1:1). We haven't! If anyone ever needed a **perfect** Bible it is us, nearly two thousand years separated from a Saviour we have **never seen!**

Why did God inspire a perfect original if He didn't plan on preserving it? Couldn't He have afforded some errors in His originals just as some believe He has allowed some errors in today's Bible? Or do critics of God's perfect Bible believe that God was unable to **prevent** errors in the copies. It would seem like only half of a God who had the power to do one but not the other.

3. It is a "convenient" faith which cannot be tested. In other words, it is rather safe to believe in a perfect set of originals which have been **LOST.** Since they are lost, no one can ever practically challenge such a belief. Adherents to such a shallow persuasion can rest safely in the fact that they will never be proven wrong since the evidence needed to prove them wrong (the "originals") is lost.

But if they dare put the same faith in a Bible available today, they know that they will definitely be bloodied defending their faith.

Thus, to believe in a perfect set of originals, but not to believe in a perfect English Bible, is to believe **nothing** at all.

4. Regardless of their arguments against the doctrine of a **preserved perfect Bible,** such a fact is as much guaranteed by Scripture as the bodily return of Jesus Christ (Acts 1:8).

Psalm 12:7 plainly states, "Thou shalt keep them, O LORD, thou shalt preserve them from this generation for ever."

Thus we have **God** promising to **preserve** the same words that He **inspired.** Not too much of a feat to overwhelm such an omnipotent Being.

The fearful fundamentalist launches two attacks on the Scriptural teaching found in Psalm 12:7.

1. They claim, "Verse 7 is talking about the Jews, not the Bible." Then to add credence to their claim they rush out and publish a translation that says just that in Psalm 12:7. Let's look at this verse in the New International Version.

"O LORD, you will keep **us** safe and protect **us** from such people forever."

This is an irresponsible and dishonest translation. The Hebrew word "shamar" meaning "to keep" which the New International Version translators render "you will keep **us**" is found in the future second person singular "thou shalt keep" and is directed to the **THIRD** person plural "them" and **NOT** the **first** person plural "us" as the New International Version translators rendered it.

Thus we see it is the King James, God's perfect, preserved Bible which has **accurately** preserved the reading of the originals, **not** the unreliable New International Version.

Psalm 12:7 is **not** God's promise to preserve the Jews, a promise which flourishes elsewhere in Scripture. It is God's promise to preserve His words, and is a direct reference to those words as described in Psalm 12:6.

2. Oftimes a Christian, whose faith is too weak to accept the literal truth of Psalm 12:6,7, will piously quote Psalm 119:89.

"For ever, O LORD, thy word is settled in heaven."

Then they will state that God actually meant that He preserved His perfect Bible in **Heaven,** not on Earth. And they say this with a straight face! This escape to a house of straw is embarrassingly humorous.

First, it is foolish for anyone to believe that God inspired a perfect original **on earth** so that He could have it brought to Heaven. Is **that** supposed to be the reason that He wrote the originals? The answer is embarrassingly simple. The **Bible** is addressed to **man**, not God. God did not write a perfect book directed to **man** and then put it in a library in Heaven where man cannot benefit from its existence. Again we ask, "What good to us, **here** and **now**, is a perfect book locked up out of reach in Heaven?"

Secondly, Psalm 12:6 makes reference to His words being on **earth**. To preserve them somewhere other than on earth is not to preserve them at all. So we see then that God **inspired** the originals perfectly. Then over the centuries He has **preserved** those same words to today. They are found in the Authorized Version.

ADDITIONAL NOTE:

In the area of "inspired translations" it might be noted that the double truth of Genesis 22:8 which in a King James Bible is plainly revealed as a prophetic reference to Jesus Christ, is lost in such weak translations as the New King James, the New International Version, and the New American Standard Version.

Question #29

QUESTION: Can a translation be inspired?

ANSWER: Yes, God has inspired several.

EXPLANATION: In the Book of Genesis, chapters 42-45, we have the record of Joseph's reunion with his brethren. That Joseph spokc Egyptian instead of Hebrew is evident by Genesis 42:23.

"And they knew not that Joseph understood them; for he spake unto them by an interpreter."

It is, of course, an accepted fact that no translation can be "word perfect". Therefore we know that the Hebrew **translation** of Joseph's Egyptian statements as found in the Old Testament manuscripts cannot be an exact word for word copy. We are left with quite a dilemma. **WHOM** did God inspire? Did He inspire Joseph's Egyptian statements, the Egyptian interpreter's verbal translation, or Moses' written translation as found in the Hebrew of the Old Testament?

If God inspired Joseph, was his "original" statement marred by his Egyptian interpreter, or by Moses' translation? Or did God inspire Moses to pen an "inspired translation" which would fly in the face of many Fundamentalist's charges of "progressive inspiration?"

This same question arises in Exodus chapters 4-14 in Moses' contest with Pharaoh. Moses, though speaking for **God** to an Egyptian king in the king's native Egyptian tongue, translates both his **and** Pharaoh's statements into Hebrew when he records the account in writing. Which did God inspire? The verbal statements made in Egyptian, a copy of which NO ONE ON EARTH HAS? Or did He inspire Moses' Hebrew translation?

The problem of inspired translations refuses to go away.

In Acts 22 Paul speaks to his Jewish tormentors in the Hebrew language (Acts 21:40, 22:2). The testimony found in verses 1 through 21 is all given orally in Hebrew. Yet there is **NO** manuscript extant of Acts 22 which records Paul's statement in Hebrew. Luke wrote it all out in Greek. Which did God inspire? Paul's verbal statement or Luke's ''progressive inspiration''?

The answer is simple and is found in II Timothy 3:16.

''All scripture is given by inspiration of God, and is profitable for doctrine, for reproof, for correction, for instruction in righteousness:''

The word ''scripture'' by its very root, ''script'' is a term for **written** words. Therefore, we can rest assured that the various translations (there are **more** than the few that I have pointed out) we have in our Bible are the **inspired** words of God. If a Fundamentalist chooses not to believe in inspired translations, he will have to do it **contrary** to the Bible **practice.**

Question #30

QUESTION: The King James Bible is a mere translation from Greek to English. A translation can't be as good as the originals, can it?

ANSWER: A translation cannot only be ''as good'' as the originals, but better.

EXPLANATION: There are three ''translations'' spoken of in the Bible. In all three cases, the translation referred to is better than the original. Since we accept the Bible as our **final** authority in all matters of faith and **practice, ITS** ''practice'' will have more authority than any ''mere human'' opinion.

1. The first translation mentioned in scripture is found in II Samuel 3:7-10..

7 ''And Saul had a concubine, whose name was Rizpah, the daughter of Aiah: and Ish-bosheth said to Abner, Wherefore hast thou gone in unto my father's concubine?

8 Then was Abner very wroth for the words of Ish-bosheth, and siad, Am I a dog's head, which against Judah do shew kindness this day unto the house of Saul thy father, to his brethren, and to his friends, and have not delivered thee into the hand of David, that thou chargest me to day with a fault concerning this woman?

9 So do God to Abner, and more also, except, as the LORD hath sworn to David, even so I do to him;

10 To translate the kingdom from the house of Saul, and to set up the throne of David over Israel and over Judah, from Dan even to Beersheba.''

After the death of King Saul in I Samuel 31, Abner, who had been the captain of Saul's army installed Ish-bosheth as King instead of David. (II Samuel 12:8,9)

Later Ish-bosheth and Abner had a falling out. Abner, in anger, announces to Ish-bosheth that he is going to "translate" the Kingdom of Israel from Ish-bosheth to David.

It is obvious by Abner's statement of II Samuel 3:9 that the LORD **wanted** David to be king over all twelve tribes of Israel. Therefore the "translation" of the kingdom of Israel to David was **BETTER** than the "original" state which had a split kingdom with David rightly ruling over one portion and Ish-bosheth wrongly ruling over the other section. (Remember the law of first mentions.)

2. The second translation spoken of in scripture is found in Colossians 1:13.

"Who hath delivered us from the power of darkness, and hath translated us into the kingdom of his dear Son:"

Here the "translation" spoken of is the conversion of a lost sinner to a new life in Jesus Christ. No one in their right mind could even **pretend** that this translation is not a massive improvement over the "original" condition.

3. The third translation found in the Bible is located in Hebrews 11:5.

"By faith Enoch was translated that he should not see death; and was not found, because God had translated him: for before his translation he had this testimony, that he pleased God."

The word "translate" only appears five times in scripture. Once in II Samuel, once in Colossians and the remaining three times here in Hebrews 11:5.

A Christian with even a shallow knowledge of the Bible is familiar with the story of Enoch from Genesis 5. Enoch walked with God and is known to have pleased God. He was a prophet (Judge 14) and a man of faith. God saw fit to **physically** take Enoch to heaven so that he would not have to experience death. This individual action is a miniature version of What Christians call "The Rapture," mentioned in I Corinthians 15, I Thessalonians 4, Titus 2 and various other places in the a Bible. Since the word "Rapture" appears nowhere in scripture a more proper name for this future occurrence might be ''The Blessed Hope'' (Titus) or ''The Catching Up'' (I Thessalonians) or ''Our Translation'' (Hebrews).

It is obvious that Enoch's translation was an improvement over his ''original'' condition.

Thus we see that every translation mentioned in our **final authority** in **all matters** is an improvement over the original.

If you are a simple Bible believer you will have no trouble accepting this. If you worship education or just hate to be wrong you will reject this Bible fact as easily as you have rejected **every** Bible fact that you couldn't agree with.

It should be noted here that the perplexed translators of both the New American Standard Version and the New International Version, when faced with this **glaring** contradiction of their own personal prejudice, could not bring themselves to allow the word ''translation'' in any of the above mentioned passages.

Which will **you** follow, the Bible or men?

Question #31

QUESTION: I can still find the fundamentals in other bibles. So how can they be bad?

ANSWER: Any fundamental found in **any** version is found purer or more frequently in the King James Bible thus making the King James Bible the best of the field.

EXPLANATION: Most people who claim to be able to find the fundamentals in other versions forget that the very fundamentals which they claim to be able to find, were originally taught them from a King James Bible.

Following are just a few doctrines which can be **found** in other versions but found in a **weaker** state than in the King James Bible. (The versions mentioned are used as a cross-section of versions available and do not necessarily include or exclude others.)

1. The deity of Christ is watered down in Acts 3:13,26, 4:27,30 in the New King James Version, the New International Version and New American Standard Version where Jesus is called God's "servant" instead of God's "Son."

2. The doctrine of Hell is watered down in Luke 16:23 in the New King James Version and New American Standard Version where they transliterate "Hades" instead of translating it as "Hell."

3. The salvation of the Ethiopian eunuch is eliminated in the New International Version and New American Standard Version where Acts 8:37 is removed from the text.

4. The Ascension of Jesus Christ is left out of Luke 24:51

in a New American Standard Version.

5. The virgin birth of Jesus is denied in the New International Version and New American Standard Version in Luke 2:33 where Joseph is called Jesus' father.

6. The doctrine of the Trinity is either removed or questioned in I John 5:7 where the New American Standard Version and New International Version remove the verse and then split verse 6 and manufacture a false verse 7 and in the New King James Version where a note casts doubt on its authenticity.

These are just a **few** corruptions in the texts of today's modern versions. It is not an exhaustive list by any means.

It may be stated that such criticism of other bibles is "nit-picking". But, let it be remembered that, if you can find a particular doctrine in a modern bible, let's say, 200 times and you can find the **same** doctrine **more** times in the King James, then the King James is stronger.

Question #32

QUESTION: If the King James is really perfect, how can so many preachers and scholars be wrong about it?

ANSWER: The majority is ALWAYS wrong.

EXPLANATION: In Matthew 7:13,14 Jesus points out a great Bible truth. The **majority** of the population will **not** get saved.

"Enter ye in at the strait gate: for wide is the gate, and broad is the way, that leadeth to destruction, and many there be which go in thereat:

Because strait is the gate, and narrow is the way, which leadeth unto life, and few there be that find it."

This passage teaches us that the majority of people on the earth at any given time will **wrongly** reject Christ and go to Hell.

Even a casual look at the Bible will show that the majority is always going to be wrong.

The **majority** of people rejected Noah's preaching and died in the flood.

The **majority** of people perished in Sodom and Gomorrah.

The **majority** of Israel worshipped Aaron's calf in Exodus 32.

The **majority** of Israel rejected the ministry of the prophets such as Jeremiah.

The **majority** of people rejected Jesus Christ during His earthly ministry.

The **majority** of people alive today reject Jesus Christ as the Saviour of the world.

It would seem that throughout history, it has always been a small group of people who have had a heart soft enough to accept God's revealed truth.

The fact that the majority of Bible "scholars" and preachers reject the King James Bible is entirely scriptural. And **WRONG.**

Question #33

QUESTION: Isn't the Holy Spirit incorrectly called "it" in Romans 8:26 in the King James Bible?

ANSWER: No. There is nothing wrong with the translation of "pneuma" in Romans 8:26.

EXPLANATION: The refutation of this popular though feeble charge against the integrity of the Bible comes from three sources. First, the Greek language itself, secondly, the hypocrisy of Bible critics and thirdly, from Jesus Christ Himself. (Since the Bible is our final authority in all matters of **faith** and **practice**, His testimony **should** hold considerable influence.)

First, the word translated "itself" in Romans 8:26 is "pneuma" which means "spirit." (Since the "spirit" is like air (Genesis 1:7, John 3:8) we use the word "pneumatic" to describe things that are air operated.) In Greek every word has its own distinct gender, masculine, feminine or neuter. Masculine gender is denoted by the article "o," feminine by "a," and neuter by "to." The word for spirit, "pneuma" is **neuter**, a fact which is known to even first year Greek language students. Thus, the King James Bible **correctly** translates pneuma "itself" because it would be grammatically incorrect to translate it "himself" as many of today's inferior translations do. Since critics of the King James Bible like to deride it for pretended "mistranslations" of the Greek, it seems hypocritical indeed to criticize it here for properly translating the Greek. Then to add insult to ignorance they laud other versions such as the New American Standard Version, New International Version, and New King James Version which INCORRECTLY render pneuma as "himself."

Secondly, in adding to their hypocrisy and exposing their disdain for God's Bible, these same critics, who become indignant at the Holy Spirit being called "it" in Romans 8 in a King James Bible, will promote translations such as the New American Standard Version and the New International Version which call God a "What" in Acts 17:23. The Authorized Version correctly renders it "Whom."

Thirdly, and most convincingly, is a statement that Jesus Christ makes in John chapter 4 while dealing with the woman at the well.

Jesus, completely unintimidated by twentieth century scholarship, doesn't hesitate to say to the woman in verse 22, "Ye worship ye know not what: we know **what** we worship: for salvation is of the Jews."

To whom is Jesus referring to by the word "what?" The next verse defines His statement perfectly.

"But the hour cometh, and now is, when the true worshipers shall worship **the Father** in spirit and in truth: for the Father seeketh such to worship him."

Thus we see that Jesus finds referring to His own Father as "what" in verse 22 a **non-issue**. While the mighty mice of twentieth century scholarship would translate an entirely new version over it. Even though they, in their own casual conversation, find no offense in referring to the Holy Spirit in the neuter.

Which will **you** follow?

Question #34

QUESTION: Didn't the King James Bible when first printed contain the Apocrypha?

ANSWER: Yes.

EXPLANATION: Many critics of the perfect Bible like to point out that the original King James had the Apocrypha in it as though that fact compromises its integrity. But several things must be examined to get the factual picture.

First, in the days in which our Bible was translated, the Apocrypha was accepted reading based on its **historical** value, though not accepted as Scripture by anyone outside of the Catholic church. The King James translators therefore placed it **between** the Old and New Testaments for its historical benefit to its readers. They did **not** integrate it into the Old Testament text as do the corrupt Alexandrian manuscripts.

That they rejected the Apocrypha as divine is very obvious by the seven reasons which they gave for not incorporating it into the text. They are as follows:

1. Not one of them is in the Hebrew language, which was alone used by the inspired historians and poets of the Old Testament.

2. Not one of the writers lays any claim to inspiration.

3. These books were never acknowledged as sacred Scriptures by the Jewish Church, and therefore were never sanctioned by our Lord.

4. They were not allowed a place among the sacred books, during the first four centuries of the Christian Church.

5. They contain fabulous statements, and statements which contradict not only the canonical Scriptures, but themselves; as when, in the two Books of Maccabees, Antiochus Epiphanes is made to die three different deaths in as many different places.

6. It inculcates doctrines at variance with the Bible, such as prayers for the dead and sinless perfection.

7. It teaches immoral practices, such as lying, suicide, assassination and magical incantation.

If having the Apocrypha **between** the Testaments disqualifies it as authoritative, then the corrupt Vaticanus and Sinaiticus manuscripts from Alexandria, Egypt must be totally worthless since their authors obviously didn't have the conviction of the King James translators and incorporated its books into the text of the Old Testament thus giving it authority with Scripture.

Question #35

QUESTION: Can someone get saved if you are using a bible other than the King James?

ANSWER: Yes.

EXPLANATION: Generally, the facts surrounding the gospel of Jesus Christ and the simplicity of salvation are found intact even in the grossest perversions of Scripture.

It must be remembered though that the Bible is a weapon in the hand of the Christian. See Hebrews 4:12, Job 40:19 and II Timothy 3:16.

It is also food that a new Christian might grow properly. See I Peter 2:2.

It is in these areas that new bibles are weakened. In fact, the very verses given above are altered in many new versions, thus weakening Scripture.

It is therefore possible to get saved through other versions, but you will never be a threat to the devil by growing.

Question #36

QUESTION: Do the Dead Sea Scrolls render the King James Bible obsolete?

ANSWER: No, they support it.

EXPLANATION: The Dead Sea Scrolls which were found by an Arab shepherd boy in 1947 in the Qumran caves near Jericho, Israel have no ill effect on the Bible.

Their text actually **agrees** with the King James Bible. This fact makes them unattractive to scholars desiring to over-throw the perfect Bible. So, other than commenting on the irony of the way in which they were found, they are largely ignored.

The translators of the King James Bible did not need the Dead Sea Scrolls since they already had the Textus Receptus which they match.

Question #37

QUESTION: What if I **really** have trouble with all of the "thee's" and "thou's" in the Bible?

ANSWER: So what? Read it anyway.

EXPLANATION: Someone once said, "God will give you a steak, but He won't cut it up and feed it to you."
Consider these facts:
God has gone to all the trouble to **inspire** the perfect originals. He has collated the books of the Old Testament and New Testament and documented their authenticity. He has **preserved** his words against attack from Roman Catholic tyrants and Alexandrian philosophers. This process has cost Him the lives, homes and families of some of His most faithful servants. He assembled the very best scholars in history and had them translate it into the world's language (English) in its absolutely purest form.
And then **YOU** gripe about the "thee's" and "thou's".
Shut up and eat your steak!

Question #38

QUESTION: The New King James Version is based on the Antiochian manuscripts. Is it an improvement over the King James Bible?

ANSWER: No.

EXPLANATION: The New King James Version is to the English Bible what the Alexandrian manuscripts are to Greek. A corruption of a **pure** text by men who hold the deplorable doctrine that the Bible cannot be perfect (**regardless** of what they may say when they preach) and must be corrected by the feeble intellect of man.

The New King James Version unlike most modern translations is based on the correct Antiochian manuscripts instead of the corrupt Alexandrian manuscripts. Unfortunately, the men doing the translation work view the Bible as imperfect. They would vehemently deny this charge in public because their jobs depend on it, but in **FACT** they do not believe that ANY Bible is perfect. **Not even their own New King James Version!** Thus, to them, the Bible is lost ("settled" in heaven) and the minds of scholars are the only hope of rescuing Its "thoughts" from oblivion.

Many of the men on the board of translators may indeed be great preachers and pastors, but that by no means entitles them to correct the Bible.

Sincerity cannot improve on perfection. Thus, instead of "making a good thing better" they have only managed, for all of their trouble, to make a "perfect thing tainted".

It must be remembered, there is a great deal of prestige in sitting on the board of translators of a ''modern'' version of the Bible (Matthew 23:5-7).

Question #39

QUESTION: Isn't the New Scofield Bible a King James Bible?

ANSWER: Not only is the New Scofield Bible **NOT** a King James Bible, it is not even a "Scofield" Bible.

EXPLANATION: The first and most weighty reason why the New Scofield Bible is not a Scofield Bible at all is shamefully simple. **Dr. C.I. Scofield did not edit it. Dr.** Scofield **died** in 1921! Barring a very "selective" resurrection, it is impossible for a man who died in 1921 to edit a book in 1967.

The publisher's justification for a new "edition" is that Dr. Scofield, whose reference Bible was first published in 1909 added material and published another edition in 1917. **But** it is an author's perogative to alter his own works, but that certainly does not give others, more than 45 years after his death, a blank check to make alterations and then sign his name to it!

If we altered the ending of "Macbeth" we would be less than honest to claim that the change met Shakespeare's approval.

Secondly, the editors exercised great liberty in changing attributes of Dr. Scofield's reference work that Dr. Scofield himself felt important enough to include in his work.

In the introduction to their doubly dishonest 1967 publication they admit such changes.

New Scofield: "Among the changes and improvements in

this edition are: important word changes in the text to help the reader; a modified system of self-pronunciation; revision of many of the introductions to the books of the Bible, including designation of the author, theme, and date; more subheadings; clarification of some footnotes, deletion of others, and the addition of many new notes; more marginal references; an entirely new chronology; a new index; a concordance especially prepared for this edition; new maps; and more legible type. Some of these features are explained below."

By their own words, they admit to altering Dr. Scofield's text (the King James Bible), introduction of books of the Bible, notes, marginal references, chronology and many other features.

Did Dr. Scofield give his approval to these changes? Not unless one of the nine committee members had the witch of Endor conjure him up as she had Samuel!

If fact, the publisher even admits that the changes made were arbitrary choices of the revision committee.

"Each position taken represents the thinking or conviction of the committee as a group."

What are the results of such shenanigans? One example will suffice. Let us examine the footnote found in Acts 8:12 of the New Scofield Bible concerning baptism.

"Baptism has, since the apostolic age, been practiced by every major group in the Christian church and, in Protestant communions, is recognized as one of two sacraments--the other being the Lord's Supper. Since early in the Church's history three different modes of baptism have been used: aspersion (sprinkling); affusion (pouring); and immersion (dipping)."

Here we see that the nine revisors (**NOT** Dr. Scofield) believe that there is a difference between the true **Christian** church and Protestant "communion". Might I ask? When **one** group is defined as "Protestant" what is the other group called?

Secondly, the nine apostate revisors (**NOT** Dr. Scofield) claim, **without scriptural proof** that Christians baptize by pouring and sprinkling as well as immersion.

Remember, the footnote is found in a S-C-O-F-I-E-L-D of

1967. A book which claims on its title page that a dead man (Dr. Scofield) is one of its editors.

What does the footnote for Acts 8:12 in the **REAL** Scofield Bible of 1917 which had a living Dr. Scofield as its editor say?

Nothing. There **IS** no such footnote!

That's right! The New "Scofield" bible has a "Scofield" note added after the death of "Scofield" the editor which the **REAL** Dr. Scofield never approved of and never had in a text anytime in his life time!

I ask you, is this honest?

Proof that the New Scofield Bible isn't a King James Bible is found on almost every page where the margin notes the twin Bible reading as "KJV". The text of the New Scofield Bible is **NOT** a King James Bible and it is NOT a Scofield Bible.

It might be noted that in recent years the size and shape of the New Scofield Bible has been changed to more resemble the Scofield Reference Bible. Many Christians who desire a true Scofield Reference Bible have purchased a New Scofield Bible **by mistake.**

The "Bible" business is lucrative. Isn't it?

Question #40

QUESTION: Is the New International Version trustworthy?

ANSWER: No.

EXPLANATION: The New International Version is based on the 26th edition of the Greek text of Eberhard Nestle published in 1979. It, like the New American Standard Version which is based on Nestle's 23rd edition of 1969, is an Egyptian bible. These and most modern translations (except the New King James Version and New Scofield Version which are handled separately in this book) are all products of Origen's tainted manuscripts from Alexandria, Egypt.

A few of the corruptions found in the New International Version and New American Standard Version are found under a previous section dealing with fundamentals. This work is by **no means** an exhaustive study of the many problems with these error riddled versions.

We suffice it to say, ''You can't get **good** fruit from a **bad** tree.'' (Matthew 7:17,18)

Question #41

QUESTION: I've heard that there have been many manuscripts discovered since 1611 that the King James translators didn't have access to. Do these strengthen or weaken the King James Bible?

ANSWER: They strengthen the King James Bible.

EXPLANATION: There have been many manuscripts found since 1611, but there have been no new **READINGS** found.

Many critics of the Word of God have used the argument of "new evidence" that the King James translators didn't have as a basis to degrade its authority. The fact is, that the King James translators had all of the **readings** available to them that modern critics have available to them today.

One of the most prominent manuscripts which has been discovered since 1611 is the Sinaitic manuscript. This witness, though horribly flawed, was found amongst trash paper in St. Cathrine's monastery at the foot of Mt. Sinai in 1841 by Constantine Tischendorf.

Sinaiticus is a sister manuscript of the corrupt manuscript, Vaticanus. Both read very similarly. So, although the Sinaitic manuscript was discovered over 200 years after the Authorized Version was translated, its **READINGS** were well known to the translators through the Vatican manuscript which was discovered in 1481 and also through the Jesuit Bible, an English translation of 1582.

So we see that there are no readings available today to

scholars which were not already in the hands of the King James translators. We might further add that an **honest** scholar will admit that this ''great number of newly discovered manuscripts'' that are trumpt abroad, agree with the Greek text of the Authorized Version rather than challenging it.

Question #42

QUESTION: Aren't modern English translations easier to understand?

ANSWER: No. Some may seem easier to **read**, but none are easier to **understand**.

EXPLANATION: One of the primary advertising gimicks used to sell modern English translations is that they will be easier to understand for the potential customers. The customer, having been assured that he/she cannot possibly understand the "old archaic" King James gratefully purchases the modern English Bible and unknowingly condemns themself to a life of biblical ignorance. Modern English translations may be easier to read but they are **not** easier to understand.

Let's look at the equation in simple terms. If the "archaic" language and the "thee's" and "thou's" of the King James Bible **really** do hamper the effectiveness of the Holy Spirit in communicating His message to the Christian, then several things should be true of one or all of the raft of modern English translations on the Bible market today.

1. If modern English translations, such as the New American Standard Version, New International Version, New King James Version, and Today's English Version were easier to understand, then the Holy Spirit's message to the Christian would flow freer and accomplish greater spiritual victories in the lives of God's people on an individual basis. Yet it is sadly evident that this is not happening.

In fact it is only **too** evident to any objective observer that today's Christians are **more** worldly and **less** dedicated to Jesus Christ than their nineteenth or even early twentieth century counterparts who were raised on and **read** the King James Bible. Surely a Bible that was "easier to understand" would have dramatically increased successes in battling sin, worldliness and carnality, but this JUST HAS NOT HAP-PENED.

2. Secondly, if the modern English translations were **really** easier to understand then I believe God would/show a little more gratitude for them by using **at least one** to/spark a major revival in this nation.

It is elementary to see that if the "old archaic" King James Bible has been hampering the **desired** work of the Holy Spirit, then God should be eager to bless the use of any translation that would be easier for his people to understand.

Again, it is all too obvious that no mass spiritual awakening of **any kind** has been initiated by any one of today's modern translations. Today's modern translations haven't been able to spark a revival in a **Christian school**, let alone be expected to close a bar.

In fact, since the arrival of our modern English translations, beginning with the ASV of 1901, America has seen:

1. God and prayer kicked out of our public school
2. Abortion on demand legalized
3. Homosexuality accepted nationally as an "alternate life style"
4. In home pornography via TV and VCR
5. Child kidnapping and pornography running rampant
6. Dope has become an epidemic
7. Satanism is on the rise

If this is considered a "revival" then let's turn back to the King James to **STOP it**.

In fact, the **ONLY** scale used to claim success for a new translation is **how well it sells**. This depraved Madison Avenue sales system should set alarms ringing in the Christian. Instead, deluded by television, they dutifully nod and remark that, "It must be good, everbody's buying one."

Is there any "good" coming from modern translations? Surely. The publishing companies are making millions.

Today American Christians are spiritually anemic. They turn instead to their favorite ''Bible psychologist'' for help rather than Scripture. America as a whole is as morally decayed as Sodom and Gomorrah.(Ezekiel 16:49).

Where is the spiritual help and hope that an ''easier to understand'' translation should bring?

Instead, perhaps we are in this desperate condition **because** of those very translations.

Question #43

QUESTION: Isn't the devil behind all the confusion and fighting over Bible versions?

ANSWER: Undoubtedly.

EXPLANATION: It is a great irony that many of the critics of the Bible claim rather indignantly that the devil is behind the battle over the King James Bible. In this they are correct. But **somehow** they have managed to assume that it is the people claiming perfection for the Bible who the devil is guiding. Is this a correct assumption? Let us consider the history of the battle.

From the time of its publication in 1611 the King James Bible has grown in popularity. Although not mandated by the King to be used in the churches of England, it did, in a matter of a few years, manage to supplant all of the great versions translated before it. Though it was not advertised in the Madison Avenue fashion of today's versions, it soon swept all other versions from the hearts and hands of the citizenry of England and its colonies.

With the conquest of the British Empire behind it, it crossed the Atlantic to the United States. Landing here it overwhelmed the double foothold of the Roman Catholic Church planted previously under the flags of Spain and France.

It then began to permeate young America with its ideals. Its truths led to the establishment of an educational system, based on Scripture, that was unparalleled in the world. It instilled in men the ideals of freedom and personal liberty, thoughts so foreign to the minds of men that their inclusion in our Constitution could only be described as an "experiment" in government.

It commissioned preachers of righteousness who, on foot and horseback, broke trails into the wilderness and spread the truth of the gospel and of right living. In its wake was left what could only be described... "one nation, **under God...**" This accomplished, it set out for the conquest of the heathen world. Bible colleges (Princeton, Harvard, Yale) were founded. Mission societies formed. And eager young missionaries began to scour the globe with little more than a King James Bible and God's Holy Spirit.

But these activities did not go unnoticed by Satan. He who had successfully counterfeited God's church, ministers and powers certainly could not be expected to let God's Bible roam the world unchallenged. Through agents such as Brook Foss Westcott and Fenton John Anthony Hort, he published his own translation in 1884. (The New Testament had been published in 1881.) Though there had been sporadic personal translations between 1611 and 1884, this new translation, called the Revised Version, was the first ever to be designed from its out set to replace God's Authorized Bible. It failed to replace God's Bible, but the arguments of its adherents were the first shots fired in a nearly 400 year battle for the hearts and minds of God's people concerning the authority and fidelity of Scripture.

In 1901 another round was fired in the form of the American Revised Version, later called the American Standard Version. (An intentional misnomer since it never became the "standard" for **anything**.) This version, other than being the darling of critical American scholarship met a dismal end when, twenty-three years later, it was so totally rejected by God's people that its copyright had to be sold. (Does this sound like God's blessing?)

The ASV was further revised and republished in 1954 as the Revised Standard Version. This sequence of events has repeated itself innumerable times, resulting in the New American Standard Version of 1960, the New Scofield Version of 1967, the New International Version of 1978, and the New

King James Version of 1979 to name a **few**.

The process has never changed. Every new version that has been launched has been, without exception, a product of Satan's Alexandrian philosophy which rejects the premise of a **perfect** Bible. Furthermore, they have been copied, on the most part, from the corrupt Alexandrian manuscript. (Although a few have been translated from pure Antiochian manuscripts after they were tainted by the Alexandrian philosophy.)

THIS then was Satan's battle in **print**, BUT by **no** means was it his exclusive onslaught. He used a standard military "two-pronged" attack.

While popularizing his Alexandrian manuscripts via the press, he began to promote his Alexandrian philosophy in and through Christian Bible colleges.

Soon sincere, naive, young, Bible students attending **FUNDAMENTAL** Bible colleges began to hear the infallibility of the Bible challenged in their classrooms. In chapel services the Bible's perfection was much touted. But then, **the very same speakers**, would debase, degrade, and even mock the English Bible, always assuring their students that they were not a "liberal" or "modernist" because they believed that the Bible was infallible in "the originals". That non-existent, unobtainable, mystical entity which ALL apostates shield their unbelief behind.

Soon stalwartness gave in to acceptance and fidelity to a perfect Bible became fidelity to one's "Alma Mater". Young graduates, disheartened and disarmed by their education, found themselves in pulpits across America parroting the professor's shameful criticism of the Word of God. They readily accepted new versions hot off the Alexandrian presses.

Then, when some Christian approached them claiming to believe the Bible (one you could **hold in your HAND**, not a lost relic from bygone days) was **word perfect** (a belief **they** had once held before their education stole it from them) they felt threatened. They try to dispel this "fanatic', this "cultist". Finally they look this faith filled Christian in the eye and piously ask, "Don't you feel that the devil is using this Bible version issue to divide and hinder the cause of Christ?"

"Undoubtedly," comes back the answer "But I'm certainly glad it's not **MY CROWD** that he's using." (!)

Who's side are **YOU** on?

Additional Note:

Here's something that you need to think about. If we King James Bible believers have our way, a Preacher would stand in a pulpit to read Scripture and everyone else in the church would read from the **same Bible.** Isn't that **UNITY?**

But if the Bible-correctors have their way everyone would read from a different bible. That's confusion. And **who** is the author of confusion? (I Cor. 14:33)

Question #44

QUESTION: Who were Westcott and Hort?

ANSWER: Two unsaved Bible critics.

EXPLANATION: Brook Foss Westcott (1825-1903) and Fenton John Anthony Hort (1828-1892) were two non-Christian Anglican ministers. Fully steeped in the Alexandrian philosophy that ''there is no perfect Bible'', they had a vicious distaste for the King James Bible and its Antiochian Greek text, the Textus Receptus. [The infidelity of Westcott and Hort is well documented in this author's work entitled An Understandable History of the Bible, 1987, Bible Believer's Press, P.O. Box 1249, Pottstown, PA. 19464]

It cannot be said that they believed that one could attain Heaven by either works or faith, since both believed that Heaven existed only **in the mind of man**.

Westcott believed in and attempted to practice a form of Communism whose ultimate goal was communal living on college campus's which he called a ''coenobium.''

Both believed it possible to communicate with the dead and made many attempts to do just that through a society which they organized and entitled ''The Ghostly Guild.''

Westcott accepted and promoted prayers for the dead. Both were admirers of Mary (Westcott going so far as to call his wife Sarah, ''Mary''),and Hort was an admirer and proponent of Darwin and his theory of evolution.

It is obvious to even a casual observer why they were well equipped to guide the Revision Committee of 1871-1881 away from God's Antiochian text and into the spell of Alexandria.

They had compiled their own Greek text from Alexandrian manuscripts, which, though unpublished and inferior to the Textus Receptus, they secreted little by little to the Revision Committee. The result being a totally new Alexandrian English Bible instead of a ''revision'' of the Authorized Version as it was claimed to be.

It has only been in recent years that scholars have examined their unbalanced theories concerning manuscript history and admitted that their agreements were weak to non-existent.

Sadly, both men died having never known the joy and peace of claiming Jesus Christ as their Saviour.

Question #45

QUESTION: Can a person of Greek ethnic origin better understand the Greek New Testament and therefore correct the English Bible?

ANSWER: No.

EXPLANATION: The Greek language as found in the New Testament and the modern Greek language spoken in Greece are so vastly different from each other as to be non-interchangeable one with the other.

The faulty assumption that a "Greek" would be equipped, due to his nationality, to change the English Bible is humorous at best and arrogant at worst.

No man, Greek or otherwise, has been inspired by God to change the Bible.

Teaching "from the Greek by a Greek" may sell many books and lead to a rich Greek, but it certainly doesn't lead to a better understanding of God's word.

Question #46

QUESTION: What is a "Ruckmanite?"

ANSWER: "Ruckmanite" is a name Bible critics call anyone who disagrees with them.

EXPLANATION: Peter Sturges Ruckman was born in 1921. He has spent years studying the manuscript history of the Bible. He received his doctorate in philosophy from Bob Jones University.

He has personally founded or helped to found dozens of churches. He is the founder and president of the Pensacola Bible Institute in Pensacola, Florida, where he has trained hundreds of preachers, missionaries and Christian laymen. He has also authored over forty books and Bible commentaries.

He is, without a doubt, the most outspoken champion of the King James Bible in this generation. He is considered an extremely dangerous foe to the Bible critics who teach that God has not preserved His Bible perfect. (In spite of Psalm 12:6,7).

His arsonal consists of an above average intellect, years of studying Bible manuscripts and a caustic delivery. This abrasive preaching style so offends (and scares) today's limpwristed "soldiers of the Lord" that they shrink from any confrontation with him, OR the facts he presents.

ALL Bible critics claim to believe that the Bible is the "perfect word of God without a mixture of error." They make this claim to deceive the people in their congregations. They live in fear that a member of their congregation will pick up one of Dr. Ruckman's many books and discover the difference between someone who "claims" to believe that the Bible is perfect and someone who really does.

Many Christians on their own, have concluded that the Bible (King James Bible) is the absolute perfect word of God. They, in complete innocence, will question their pastor's "improvements" on scripture and suddenly find themselves denounced as "Ruckmanite." In many cases they have never even heard of Dr. Peter S. Ruckman.

This denunciation is a simple yet desperate tactic. No Christian wants to be guilty of "following a man." Therefore, the Bible critic reasons that if Bible believers can be accused of "man following" they will discard their conviction and humbly follow them.

I once met a preacher who rejected the thought of being grouped with Bible believers because he would then be a "Ruckmanite." He claimed, "I don't follow any man."

This sounds very pious. He later informed me that he was a "Calvinist." (A follower of the teachings of the man, John Calvin).

So, today, anyone who really believes that the Bible is the perfect word of God without a mixture of error AND can produce it instead of just talk about it can expect to be called a "Ruckmanite" by someone who feels threatened by their faith and confidence.

Question #47

QUESTION: What about "nuggets" found only in the Greek?

ANSWER: Why settle for "nuggets" when you can own the whole mine?

EXPLANATION: Most "nuggets" that Preachers find in the Greek exist only in the fantasy of their minds.

First, anyone who believes that the Bible is the perfect word of God, **cannot** believe that it can be improved on... **even** by them. Most men who discover "nuggets" are filled with a prideful humility through which they believe that God is going to show **them** something in the Greek that no one else has found. Then they can "humbly" impress their preacher friends with their monumental "grasp" of the original language.

They do not, regardless of what they say in the pulpit, really believe that the Bible is perfect as it stands, in English **OR** Greek. Therefore they never read their Bible with a desire for the Holy Spirit to help them understand it. They instead "pray" that He will show them some better way to translate some Greek word.

Since the Holy Spirit never does this, they usually resort to "The Greek Game". This game can be played by **anyone**. Even if they have had no training in the Greek language. Simply put, all that the pseudo-scholar needs to do is to own a Young's Concordance. In the very back of a Young's Concordance is a list of the Greek and Hebrew words used in

124

the Bible. Under each word given is a list of the different ways that that particular word was translated in the King James Bible. All the eager critic needs to do is to interchange the English words used.

For example, take the Greek word "haplotes." It was translated five different ways in the Authorized Version.

1. bountifulness   II Corinthians 9:11
2. liberal   II Corinthians 9:13
3. liberality   II Corinthians 8:2
4. simplicity   Romans 12:8, II Corinthians 1:12
5. singleness   Ephesians 6:5, Colossians 3:22

Now, in order for our zealous scholar to humbly display his massive intellect, he must find a verse where "haplotes" is translated, let's say, "singleness" or way #5. Such as Ephesians 6:5.

"Servants, be obedient to them that are your masters according to the flesh, with fear and trembling, in singleness of your heart, as unto Christ;"

Then in his preaching, when lighting upon his prearranged "victim" he makes some statement that is **critical** of the King James translators for having poorly chosen this translation. Then he chooses one of the other words into which it was translated, say, way #3 or #4 and takes 10-15 minutes to expound on the virtues of his choice while ever pointing out sadly the poor choice of the Authorized Version translators. Of course, later when he reads a verse such as Romans 12:8, "Or he that exhorteth, on exhortation: he that giveth, let him do it with **simplicity**; he that ruleth, with diligence; he that sheweth mercy, with cheerfulness.", where his pet Greek word is translated "simplicity" or way #4, he will reverse the process and expound on the virtue of choice #5. All the time lamenting, again, the poor choice of God's translators.

His audience, unaware of the ease with which this is accomplished, stares on in awe of his intelligence and tremendous grasp of the Greek language. They feel so fortunate to have a man of such caliber (.22 Blank!) to point out to them the errors in their Bible. And of course they are totally convinced by this charade that they, lowly peons that they are, can **never** truly understand the Bible as well as their exalted teacher, because they lack the "tools" he possesses from the Greek.

This scenario is **NOT** an over statement. I have experienced it first hand.

Once while listening to a self-impressed Bible scholar preach I marveled at the ease with which he duped his audience. He was reading Romans chapter 8. Upon reading a particular verse, he stopped at a particular word and stated, "Now the King James translators mistranslated the Greek word used here." Then he spent 10-12 minutes expounding on the merits of **his** choice of translation. The audience was duly impressed with this man's grasp of the "original language." (I once heard a 14 year old boy do the same thing in a "preaching contest". You see, **ANYONE** can do it!)

The very next day I was listening to another preacher on the radio. Coincidentally this zealot was also preaching from Romans chapter 8. He **also** read the same verse and **ALSO** stopped at the very same word that the expert from the previous evening had accosted. He then stated, "Sadly, the King James translators did not properly translate the Greek word used here."

I then braced myself for a rehash of the previous evening's exposition. But it was not to be. For **this** particular scholar pointed out that the word in question should have been translated an entirely different way (choice #1 vs. choice #4).

He then, as the previous evening's butcher, expounded on the virtues of **HIS** choice over that of the King James translators, **or** last evening's expert. I was amazed! Two completely different men, two entirely different opinions. In fact, their **only** point of agreement was that the **Bible** could not possibly be **correct** as it was. I quickly consigned their esteemed (and humble) opinions to the garbage heap of education and accepted the choice that **GOD** had made for His Book in 1611.

A second method of finding "nuggets" is for someone with a limited understanding of Greek to do the same as the above, only they take their choice of words from the Greek Lexicon instead of the Concordance.

The result is always the same, the congregation is overwhelmed by the "depth" of his study. They are also convinced that they can never match his comprehension of the Bible without matching (Ha!) his comprehension of "the Greek."

A tremendous example of the fallacy of this method of Bible (?) study is recorded in Dr. David Otis Fuller's book entitled <u>Which</u> <u>Bible?</u>] We quote it in its entirety.

"An interesting story is found in Walton's biography of Bishop Sanderson illustrating the truth of the old proverb, "a little learning is a dangerous thing." Dr. Kilbye, an excellent Hebrew scholar and Professor of this language in the university, also expert in Greek and chosen as one of the translators, went on a visit with Sanderson, and at church on Sunday they heard a young preacher waste a great amount of the time allotted for his sermon in criticizing several words in the then recent translation. He carefully showed how one particular word should have been translated in a different way. Later that evening the preacher and the learned strangers were invited together to a meal, and Dr. Kilbye took the opportunity to tell the preacher that he could have used his time more profitably. The Doctor then explained that the translators had very carefully considered the "three reasons" given by the preacher, but they had found another thirteen more weighty reasons for giving the rendering complained of by the young critic."

A third type of "nugget" is one which actually does not exist except in totally false statements made by a Bible critic.

The greatest example of this is found in the analogy of the two Greek words "agape" and "phileo". Both of which are translated "love" in John 21:15-17.

15 *"So when they had dined, Jesus saith to Simon Peter, Simon, son of Jonas, lovest thou me more than these? He saith unto him, Yea, Lord; thou knowest that I love thee. He saith unto him, Feed my lambs.*

16 *He saith to him again the second time, Simon, son of Jonas, lovest thou me? He saith unto him, Yea, Lord: thou knowest that I love thee. He saith unto him, Feed my sheep.*

17 *He saith unto him the third time, Simon, son of Jonas, lovest thou me? Peter was grieved because he said unto him the third time, Lovest thou me? And he said unto him, Lord,*

thou knowest all things; thou knowest that I love thee. Jesus saith unto him, Feed my sheep."

We have all heard this passage expounded by a pseudo-scholar. (Sometimes in complete sincerity due to acceptance of bad teaching.) The presentation is made that "agape" in Greek speaks of a deep, intimate, selfless love. "Phileo" on the other hand is little more than a casual "friendly" type of love. Our scholar then laments, almost tearfully, the constraints of the English language. He points out that the Lord actually says, "Peter...lovest ("agape") thou me. (With a deep, intimate, selfless love) more than these?"

Peter responds, "Yea, Lord; thou knowest that I love ("phileo") thee." (With a casual, friendly type of love.)

Our Bible critic points out that the Lord, not receiving the answer that He desires, asks again.

"Simon, son of Jonas, lovest ("agape") thou me?"

Peter, it is then pointed out, is unwilling to commit himself to such a deep relationship so he responds again.

"Yea, Lord; thou knowest that I love ("phileo") thee."

At this point our Bible corrector points out that a saddened Saviour gives in to Peter's lack of commitment and changes His own choice of Greek words to "phileo".

"Simon, son of Jonas, lovest ("phileo") thou me?"

This sudden change supposedly shocks Peter into seeing his own spiritual infidelity to the Lord. Thus, saddened he answers.

"... thou knowest that I love ("phileo") thee."

Our false teacher then points out to his audience that there is no way to attain such depth of meaning from this passage using only the feeble English. Once more the trusty "Greek" has enlightened us as English can never do!

This presentation is tremendously effective and has only **ONE** flaw. The definitions given for "agape" and "phileo" are **TOTALLY UNTRUE!**

I am about to make a statement concerning "agape" and "phileo" which is not based on prejudice or opinion. It is based on careful honest study of the way in which "agape" and "phileo" were **used in the Bible** ("Our final authority in all matters of faith and **practice**) by Jesus Christ Himself and the New Testament writers.

The statement is this: There was absolutely NO DIFFER-ENCE in New Testament times between "agape" and "phileo" and that **BOTH** are used interchangeably by Jesus Christ and the writers of the New Testament. **REGARDLESS** of what Greek grammars, Greek teachers and Greek preachers may say!

If you have been steeped in the false teaching of "agape" and "phileo" by your college professor or pastor, you will immediately (and with much prejudice) reject my supposi-tion. ("How could such godly men be wrong?" Right?)

Yet, I will not attempt to prove it is true. The proof will come from Jesus Christ,Paul, Peter and John, and any other New Testament writer that I could have chosen for the comparison. But **wait!** They are not my final witnesses. The final and most weighty argument will be waged by **YOU!**

For years I have been giving a test in Bible Conferences in which I speak concerning this false teaching of "agape" and "phileo". A copy of this test is reproduced below. **IF** you have the courage and **IF** you can be honest with God and yourself, feel free to take it. Here's how it goes.

In part #I, I have reproduced quotes from the New Testa-ment which were made by Jesus Christ using "agape" and "phileo". **Without** looking at a Greek New Testament or Concordance or any other help, use the false rules for "agape" and "phileo" given by critics of the English Bible. Read the quote. Decide whether Jesus is referring to "agape" love (deep, intimate, selfless love) or "phileo" love (casual, friendly love). Then put an "A" for agape or "P" for phileo in the blank before the quote.

Part #II is identical to part #I except that the quotes are taken from various New Testament writers. Do the same as in part one, putting an "A" for agape and a "P" for phileo, using **only** the critics definition of these words. No guessing, no hunches. Use only their own rule.

After you have completed the test, turn to the answer sheet found in Appendix #1 in the back of this book.

JOHN 21:15-17 - AGAPE vs PHILEO

INSTRUCTIONS:
1. Read the Bible quote.
2. Put an A or P in the blank before the quote to signify your choice of the Greek word used, AGAPE or PHILEO.

DEFINITIONS:
AGAPE love: Deep, intimate, selfless love.
PHILEO love: Casual "friendly" love.

I - Comparison: How **Jesus** used AGAPE and PHILEO.

_____	1.	Luke 11:42	*the love of God*
_____	2.	John 5:42	*the love of God*
_____	3.	Matt 10:37	*He that loveth father or mother*
_____	4.	Rev 3:9	*to know that I have loved*
_____	5.	Rev 3:19	*As many as I love*
_____	6.	Matt 23:6	*love the uppermost rooms*
_____	7.	John 12:25	*He that loveth his life*
_____	8.	Luke 11:43	*ye love the uppermost seats*
_____	9.	John 5:20	*the Father loveth the Son*
_____	10.	John 16:27	*the Father Himself loveth you, because ye have loved me*

II - Comparison: How **other New Testament writers** used AGAPE and PHILEO.

_____	1.	II Tim 3:4	*of pleasures more than of God*
_____	2.	John 11:5	*Jesus loved Martha*
_____	3.	John 20:2	*the other disciples whom Jesus loved*
_____	4.	I Cor 16:22	*If any man love not the Lord*
_____	5.	Rom 5:8	*But God commendeth his love*
_____	6.	I Cor 16:24	*My love be with you all*
_____	7.	II Tim 1:7	*of power, and of love, and...*
_____	8.	Rom 12:10	*one to another with brotherly love*
_____	9.	II Thes 3:12	*abound in love one toward another*

_____ 10. Titus 2:4   *women to be sober, to love their husbands*
_____ 11. Eph 5:28   *So ought men to love their wives*
_____ 12. I Peter 2:17 *Love the brotherhood*
_____ 13. Heb 13:1   *Let brotherly love continue*
_____ 14. Titus 3:4   *and love of God our Saviour*
_____ 15. I John 2:5   *in him verily is the love of God perfected*

If you have taken the test and if you have been **honest**, you have found that the **TRUTH** of the matter is that neither Jesus nor any of the New Testament writers acknowledged the false rule foisted on us by heady and high-minded Bible critics.

Thus we see that this little ''nugget'' is made only of ''FOOL'S GOLD'' and has never **really** existed except in the deluded minds of men.

Who will you believe? Jesus Christ or your Greek professor?

Question #48

QUESTION: The Textus Receptus didn't appear until 1633 so how can the King James Bible, which was translated in 1611, be translated from it?

ANSWER: Wrong.

EXPLANATION: The Greek text which was used for the translation of the King James Bible extends back through history to the pens of Moses, David, Paul, John and the other inspired writers. Throughout history it has been known by a variety of names. Over the years the Greek text of the New Testament was collated by a number of different editors. The most famous of these being Desiderius Erasmus, Theodore Beza, Robert Stephanus and the Elzevir brothers, Abraham and Bonaventure.

Erasmus published five editions of the New Testament. The first in 1516 was followed by another in 1519 which was used by Martin Luther for his historic and earth shaking German translation. His third, fourth, and fifth followed in 1522, 1527 and 1535. Erasmus' work was magnificent and set the standard for centuries (sic) to come.

Robert Stephanus published four editions, dating from 1546 through 1549, 1550 and lastly 1551.

Theodore Beza published several editions of the Greek New Testament. Four were published in 1565, 1582, 1588 and 1598. These were printed in folio, meaning a sheet of paper was folded over once, thus producing four separate pages of the book. He also published five octavo editions, these dates being; 1565, 1567, 1580, 1590 and 1604. "Octavo" means that one printed sheet folded in such a way as to produce eight separate pages of the text. Books printed in this manner tended to have a smaller page size than folio works, but sometimes led to the need of a work being printed in two or more volumes. It is Beza's edition of 1598 and Stephanus edition of 1550 and 1551 which were used as the primary sources by the King James translators.

Some years later, the Elzevir brothers published three editions of the Greek New Testament. The dates being; 1624, 1633 and 1641. They followed closely the work of Beza, who in turn had followed the standard set by Erasmus. In the preface to their edition of 1633 they coined a phrase which was to become so popular as to be retrofitted to texts which preceded it by many years. They stated in Latin "textum ergo habes, nunc ab omnibus receptum..." ei "According to the **text** now held from the volume **received**..." Thus the title "Textus Receptus" or "Received Text" was born.

So we see that, even though the name "Textus Receptus" was coined twenty-two years after the Authorized Version was translated, it has become synonymous with the true Greek Text originating in Antioch.

(For your convenience, Appendix #2 in the back of this book lists the many names used to describe both the Antiochian and Alexandrian texts.)

Question #49

QUESTION: Is it true that the King James translators were nothing but a bunch of Episcopalian baby sprinklers?

ANSWER: No.

EXPLANATION: The company of men who did the translating of the Authorized Version was made up of Bible believing men from both the Anglican and Puritan churches. Their character and qualifications have been attested earlier.

Such a statement as, "The King James translators were nothing but a bunch of Episcopalian baby sprinklers," is one of those statements which is sadly not based on fact nor conviction. It is made with the hope of character assassination and an ultimate hope of overthrowing the authority of the King James Bible in the minds of believers.

It might be beneficial at this point to note what the King James translators were NOT.

They were not adulterers, as David. Nor were they murderers as Moses and David. Nor had any of them sacrificed any of their children to Chemosh or Molech as Solomon had in I Kings 11. Nor had they vehemently denied the Lord as Peter.

These short comings are not pointed out to bring disrespect on any of the writers of scripture. But are noted so that we should be a little more gracious in our description of the men whom God has chosen to use.

Question #50

QUESTION: Believing that the King James Bible is the perfect Word of God is contrary to the stand that my "Alma Mater" takes. What should I do?

ANSWER: You should be loyal to God, Who **SHOULD** be a little higher on your "loyalty list" than your college.

EXPLANATION: First, let's get it straight. You **do not have an "Alma Mater."** The term "Alma Mater" results from the combination of the Hebrew word for "virgin" (almah) and the Greek word for "mother" (meter). Thus when you speak of your "Alma Mater" you refer to your "Virgin Mother," a terminology which we fairly say can only be used by Jesus Christ. Thus, although we may have to use the more lengthy description "the college I attended" or just "my college," we show much more respect for Jesus Christ than to go around claiming that **we** have a "Virgin Mother" **also.**

Secondly, you should appreciate the time, trouble and effort that your college went through to educate you. Education does **not** happen by accident, thus you should be appreciative of what was done on your behalf.

Thirdly, "appreciation" taken into consideration, you do not owe your **SOUL** to your college as you do to Jesus Christ. Therefore you need not be "eternally grateful" to it in such a humiliating manner that you are not allowed to control your own convictions once you graduate.

The receipt of "Dear Preacher Boy" letters from the

college President designed to pressure and intimidate you into "towing the college line" should carry no more weight than the 3rd class "Dear Occupant" mail which we all receive.

Jesus said, "The truth shall make you **FREE**" and any school which is constantly reminding you of your "debt" to them for "all we've done for you" is **not** interested in your freedom, but your slavery. You needn't feel any guilt in "respectfully" disregarding both their request and the claims.

Furthermore, if you went to a school where you paid your tuition, your room and board, and the other associated costs of your education, then you are totally free of any so called "debt" to your school. You may wholeheartedly **appreciate** the "sacrifice, vision, dedication, etc." of your school and its leaders, but your **DEBT** to it ended when you made your final tuition payment. Your degree was not given to you as a gift to show their benevolence. It was **EARNED** by your academic efforts and **PAID FOR** by your cold cash, not to mention a little "sacrifice, vision and dedication of your own.

Your college did not give you your degree because it thought that it would be a "nice" gesture. They gave it to you because **they could not refuse to**. You had EARNED it by fulfilling the requirements that they demanded. Including paying you bill. (**Plus interest** in some cases.)

Thus if you find that the perfect Bible that your school **spoke of** really does exist, and you fear being alienated from your college and its "alumni", (Greek - "enlightened ones"?) then you should remember that your debt to Jesus Christ is REAL while your "debt" to your college is only imagined.

Which do you prefer to be alienated from, Jesus Christ or your college? They are **NOT** one in the same.

John 8:32.

Question #51

QUESTION: Isn't it "Progressive Revelation" to believe that the King James Bible is to be trusted more than the originals?

ANSWER: No.

EXPLANATION: The term "Progressive Revelation" is another one of those tactics used by Bible critics to intimidate Bible believers into surrendering their faith in God's perfect Bible.

Their argument is: "Inspiration ended with the original autographs, therefore to believe that a mere translation can reveal more than the originals is to believe in a 'new' revelation, which is called 'Progressive Revelation'."

Is there such a thing as "Progressive Revelation?" Of course, we cannot afford to settle the matter on the weight of prejudice, opinion or "conviction." Only our **"final authority"** can officially dictate what is or is not proper to believe.

The obvious question then is: "Is there an example of 'Progressive Revelation' in the Bible?" The answer is: "No, there are at least two."

Moses, in the book of Exodus, goes before Pharaoh to demand the release of the children of Israel. He performs signs and wonders to prove that he truly represents God. Early in the contest Pharaoh's magicians endeavor to match Moses "miracle for miracle." (Exodus 7:11,12,22 and 8:7). We know that Pharaoh's principal two magicians were Jannes and Jambres. **BUT**, those two names are not found **anywhere** in the forty-eight chapters of the book of Exodus. Neither are they named anywhere in any one of the thirty-nine books of the Old Testament. **In fact**, their names are not **revealed** (''revelation'') until some fifteen centuries later. Could we not call that ''Progressive Revelation?''

Next let us look to I Kings 17:1. In this Old Testament verse we find that Elijah prophesies that ''there shall not be dew nor rain these years, but according to my word.'' In I Kings 18:41 ''according to his word'' Elijah lifts the three and one-half year drought from Israel. But wait. Did I say ''three and one-half year'' drought? Nowhere in I Kings is the length of time of the drought mentioned. In fact, we don't learn the length of Elijah's drought until Jesus tells us in Luke 4:25 that it was ''three years and six months.'' (This information is repeated in James 5:17). Once again we see that one portion of an occurence is recorded in the Old Testament while the remainder of the information is revealed centuries later in the New Testament. Rather ''progressive.'' Wouldn't you say?

So we see that the Bible the critic's ''boogyman'' is indeed a **Bible** teaching.

By the way, if you want to know what kind of rock Moses smote in Exodus 17:6, **don't** look for the answer in Exodus. Read Psalm 114.

Question #52

QUESTION: I've been told that believing that the King James Bible is the perfect word of God is not the "historic position." Is this true?

ANSWER: The "historic" position is to accept Scripture as infallible and deplore anyone who tries to alter it.

EXPLANATION: One of the arguments that the Roman Catholic Church uses in making its claim as the "true" church is the authority of "tradition." The Roman Catholic Church claims that tradition is equal with Scripture. This became official church dogma in 1545 at the Council of Trent. At this council, tradition was elevated to a place of equal authority with Scripture. Then the council officially cursed anyone who did not accept its tenets.

Unfortunately, "fundamental" Bible correctors have the same innate Roman Catholic tendency to resort to the "authority" of tradition. Strangely enough they do it for the very same reason. Usurping authority over Scripture. Of course, the fundamental Bible corrector realizes that the moment he uses the word "tradition" from his pulpit that "alarms" will sound in the heads of his congregation. So he shrewdly resorts to a "translation." Instead of saying "tradition" he says "the historic fundamental position is..." and completely fools his audience. What **is** a "historic position?" It is a **tradition** of course.

Therefore, when you hear someone flee to the feeble argument that "believing the King James Bible is perfect is not the historic fundamental position'', **BEWARE**. You have just run into a person who is Roman Catholic **in spirit**. If you doubt this, disagree with him and see if he doesn't curse you.

Question #53

QUESTION: Should we make an issue of Bible translations?

ANSWER: Only if you believe anything **out** of it.

EXPLANATION: Many Christians attempt to evade the issue of whether or not there really **is** a **perfect** Bible (as they are told from the pulpit) by piously hiding behind the statement, "I don't make an **issue** of Bible translations."

It is perfectly acceptable to assume such a position as long as you are **consistent** in your stand... or lack of it.

In other words, if the issue of a **perfect Bible** is a "non-issue" with you, then to be **consistent**, neither should be ANY of the following:

1. The virgin birth of Jesus Christ. *Isa 7:14*
2. The deity of Jesus Christ. *I John 5:5*
3. The substitutionary death for sins made by Jesus Christ. *Romans 5:8*
4. The bodily resurrection of Jesus Christ. *I Cor 15:4*
5. Salvation by grace alone without works. *Eph 2:8,9*
6. The Pre-millennial return of Jesus Christ. *I Thess 4*
7. The existence of a literal Heaven. *John 3:13*
8. The existence of a literal Hell. *Mark 9:42-44*
9. The acceptance of Creation over the theory of evolution. *Gen 1:1*

This is by no means a comprehensive list of convictions held by those who call themselves "Fundamentalists." Yet every one is taken **from the Bible**. How on earth can a thinking, rational person make an issue or have a conviction on something that they have taken **out** of the Bible, but see "no issue" concerning the perfection of the Book on which they base their every issue? IF the Bible has mistakes in it, then how can we be sure that it is correct in those passages on which we base our convictions?

Some may say, "I accept the Bible where it is accurately translated." Fine! **THAT** is the statement of faith of every **Mormon** in the world! **WHO** is to judge just **where** the Bible is "accuratel translated?"

No, it is impossible to make "any issue" over even **one** doctrine from the Bible and claim not to make an "issue" over the Bible itself.

Why then do people make such a statement? Basically, it is out of fear of the consequences of such a stand. They are afraid of the rejection of their friends, family, and fellow-workers.

How bold for the truth are you?

Question #54

QUESTION: Shouldn't we respect the education of our many "Drs." in the issue of the Bible?

ANSWER: Yes. **IF** there is any education associated with their degree.

EXPLANATION: Today's Christianity proliferates with "Doctors." It has often been joked that,''There are so many Doctors that you'd think God was sick.''

There are only two types of Doctor's degrees. Earned and Honorary.

An **earned** doctorate is an educational degree. It is bestowed on a graduate by his college or university upon his fulfillment of that school's requirements for such a degree. This involves certain academic achievements and acknowledges the graduate's mastery of a broad field of knowledge. Some common earned degrees are:

    M.D.   Doctor of Medicine
    Ph.D. Doctor of Philosophy
    Th.D. Doctor of Theology
    Ed.D. Doctor of Education

An **honorary** doctorate is just that. It is bestowed upon the recipient by some college or university as a way of honoring him or her for some outstanding merit, or service to that school. It must be remembered though that an honorary degree **cannot** bestow an "instant" expertise in the area named, any more than bestowing a degree on Dorothy's "Scare Crow" gave him a brain. The recipient of an honorary degree would know no more about Bible manuscripts **after** he received his degree than **before** he did. It is an **honor** only, not an academic degree. (No one would wish to be operated on by a surgeon with an "honorary" degree.) Their opinion on Bible questions certainly wouldn't outweigh the findings of an earned degree. Or even of someone who holds **no** degree but has thoroughly investigated all of the available evidence. Academically, an honorary doctorate is like an "honorary black belt" in karate. Wear it around the house, but don't try to **use** it or you'll get killed!

Some common honorary degrees are:

D.D.   Doctor of Divinity
D.Mus. Doctor of Music
D.Sc.   Doctor of Science
L.H.D. Doctor of Human Letters
Lit.D.   Doctor of Literature (or D.Lit.)
L.L.D.   Doctor of Laws
Litt.D. Doctor of Letters

Both types of degrees have their place. The honorary degree is very much a badge of merit, and should be respected as just that. An honor bestowed upon the individual for his meritorious deeds performed for Christ or his school.

The earned degree is an academic title and stands on the merit of the education that it represents.

Question #55

QUESTION: Shouldn't we emphasize love for Jesus Christ rather than squabbling over Bible translations?

ANSWER: There is no better way to emphasize our love for Jesus Christ than to jealously and zealously guard His word.

EXPLANATION: You can show your "love" for the Lord Jesus Christ in two ways.

1. Any method that **YOU** deem as sincere and valid in your own sight. (See Lev. 10:1-3)

2. You can endeavor to keep Christ's **Scriptural** admonitions as strictly as possible. (This tends to be a **lifetime** endeavor.)

In John 14:23 one of the identifying marks of anyone who **loves** Him is that they will "keep my **words**."

You may say, "That just means to keep the things that He said to do." BUT, the fact is that no "**love**" is required to keep His sayings as evidenced in John 8:51 and 52. **Love** is required to keep His "words."

Again an argument may be made that, "That just referred to the original Greek." But alas, such a statement only leads you into a deeper more deadly trap. The following **Scriptural** example will explain.

In the book of Jonah, it is recorded that Jonah, while running from God, is swallowed by "a great fish." (Jonah 1:17)

In Matthew 12:40 the "great fish" is identified by Jesus

145

Christ as a "whale." (We are not arguing genetics here, we are arguing the value of Christ's "w-o-r-d-s.")

Strangely, at this very scripture, those who claim to be able to "love" Christ and correct His Bible steal the **words** right out of His mouth.

Every new translation changes **Jesus** word "whale" to "fish." This is done because they learned in their seventh grade Biology class that "a whale is not a fish." Faced not only with a Bible that has a seeming counterdiction (not with itself but with their 7th grade Biology teacher) but also with a Saviour who is so uninformed and uneducated as to not **know** that "a whale is not a fish," they panic. They rush to Matthew 12:40 and remove the word "whale" from both the Bible (their "authority in all matters of faith and practice") and from Jesus' lips (their "Lord" and Saviour.)

The Greek word used for "whale" in Matthew 12:40 is "ketos." The Greek word for "fish" is "ichthus." They are **NOT** the same. Jesus used the Greek word "ichthus" in several places in Scripture, such as: Matthew 7:10 and 17:28. Certainly He could have used it in Matthew 12:40 if He so desired.

The fundamental Bible "enhancer" overlooks two monumental Scriptural truthes.

First he overlooks the fact that Jonah was swallowed by a "great fish" that was specially "**prepared**" by **God**. It should be noted here that Adam gave names to all living creatures but **one**. **God** gave whales their name in Genesis 1:21 BEFORE Adam named the rest of creation in Genesis 2:19,20. That means the whale had a "pre-destination" (Gen. 1:21) and a "pre-destination" (Jonah 1:17) from the **foundation** of the earth. **NOT** something even a Bible corrector should take lightly.

The second truth ignored by God's little "helper" is that by changing "whale" to "fish" in Jesus statement of Matthew 12:40 he is guilty of breaking Jesus admonition of John 14:23 to "keep my w-o-r-d-s." ("Correcting" the Bible is like "treading" quicksand. The harder you kick, the faster you sink.)

Thus the authors of the New American Standard Version,

the New International Version, the New King James Version and the rest of the new translations are not only wrong in their translation of ''ketos'' but in their defiance of Jesus mandate of John 14:23.

So, when Jesus says one thing (whale) and your Pastor, parent, or professor says another (fish) you are bound by **LOVE** for Christ to reject man's opinion and embrace and defend Jesus' w-o-r-d-s.

Question #56

QUESTION: What should I do where my Bible and my Greek Lexicon contradict?

ANSWER: Throw out the Lexicon.

EXPLANATION: Oftimes a critic of God's Bible will point to a Lexicon or Greek grammar book for authority in an effort to prove that a word has been mistranslated in the Bible. This is rather foolhardy, and flies in the face of their purported claim to accept the **Bible** as their final authority in all matters of faith and practice.

It must be remembered that God **never** claimed that He would provide us with a perfect lexicon or an inerrant Greek grammar. He said that He would provide us with a perfect **Bible**.

Thus, on the weight of our own acceptance of the Bible as our "final authority in all matters of **faith** and **practice**" we must all accept **its** rendering of the Greek as more accurate and authoritative than the **opinion** of the fallible human authors of our Greek study guides.

Question #57

QUESTION: Was Erasmus, the editor of the Textus Receptus, a ''good'' Roman Catholic?

ANSWER: Erasmus, who edited the Greek text which was later to be known as the Textus Receptus, was an embarrassment to the pope and a poor example of a ''good'' Roman Catholic.

EXPLANATION: Desiderius Erasmus was born in 1466 and died in 1536 at the age of seventy. This was no mean feat during the days when the plagues, coupled with primeval medical practices, worked together to limit the average age of a man's life to approximately 35-40 years.

Both of his parents fell victim to that same plague while Erasmus was just a lad. He and his brother were then placed in the care of an uncle who promptly sent them off to a monastery just to be rid of them. Thus Erasmus's destiny was sealed long before he could ever have a say in the matter.

Young Erasmus became well known for his charm, urbanity and wit, and was in possession of an obviously above average intellect. He was later to choose to be an Augustinian on the sole attribute that they were known to have the finest of libraries.

His behavior was somewhat bizarre by Augustinian standards. He refused to keep vigils, never hesitated to eat meat on Fridays, and though ordained, chose never to function as a priest. The Roman Church had captured his body, but quite apparently his mind and heart were still unfettered.

He is known to history as one of the most prolific writers of all times.

Erasmus was a constant and verbal opponent of the many excesses of his church. He berated the papacy, the priesthood and the over indulgences of the monks. He stated that the monks would not touch money, but that they were not so scrupulous concerning wine and women. He constantly attacked clerical concubinage and the cruelty with which the Roman Catholic Church dealt with so called "heretics." He is even credited with saving a man from the Inquisition.

One of his many writings consisted of a tract entitled "Against the Barbarians" which was directed against the overt wickedness of the Roman Catholic Church.

He was a constant critic of Pope Julius and the papal monarchy. He often compared the crusade leading Pope Julius to Julius Caesar. He is quoted as saying, "How truly is Julius playing the part of Julius." He also stated, "This monarchy of the Roman pontiff is the pest of Christendom." He advised the church to "get rid of the Roman See." When a scathing satire, in which Pope Julius was portrayed as going to Hell, written in anonymity was circulated, it was fairly common knowledge that its author was Erasmus.

He was offered a bishopric in hopes that it would silence his criticism. He rejected the bribe flat.

Erasmus published five editions of the New Testament in Greek. They were brought out successively in 1516, 1519, 1522, 1527 and 1535. His first two editions did not contain I John 5:7 although the reading had been found in many non-Greek texts dating back as early as 150 A.D. Erasmus desired to include the verse but knew the conflict that would rage if he did so without at least one Greek manuscript for authority. Following the publication of his second edition, which like his first consisted of both the Greek New Testament and his own Latin translation, he said that he would include I John 5:7 in his next edition if just **one** Greek manuscript could be found which contained it. Opponents of the reading today erringly charge that the two manuscripts found had been specially produced just to oblige Erasmus's request, but this charge has never been validated and was not held at the time of Erasmus's work.

The Roman Catholic Church criticized his works for his refusal to use Jerome's Latin translation, a translation that he said was inaccurate. He opposed Jerome's translation in two vital areas.

He detected that the Greek text had been corrupted as early as the fourth century. He knew that Jerome's translation had been based solely on the Alexandrian manuscript, Vaticanus, written itself early in the fourth century.

He also differed with Jerome on the translation of certain passages which were vital to the claimed authority of the Roman Catholic Church.

Jerome rendered Matthew 4:17 thus:''Do penance, for the kingdom of Heaven is at hand.''

Erasmus differed with:''Be penitent for the kingdom of heaven is at hand.''

Erasmus was also a staunch defender of both Mark 16:9-21 and John 8:1-12. Zeal which our modern day scholars cannot seem to find.

Possibly Erasmus's greatest gift to mankind was his attitude toward the common man. In the rigidly ''classed'' society in which he lived, he was an indefatigable advocate of putting the Scripture in the hands of the common man. While Jerome's Latin had been translated at the bidding of the Roman hierarchy, Erasmus translated his Latin with the express purpose of putting it into the hands of the common people of his day. A practice that the Roman Catholic Church knew could be dangerous to its plan to control the masses.

Erasmus is quoted as saying, ''Do you think that the Scriptures are fit only for the perfumed?'' ''I venture to think that anyone who reads my translation at home will profit thereby.'' He boldly stated that he longed to see the Bible in the hands of ''the farmer, the tailor, the traveler and the Turk.'' Later, to the astonishment of his upper classed colleagues, he added ''the masons, the prostitutes and the pimps'' to that declaration.

Knowing his desire to see the Bible in the hands of God's common people, it seems not so surprising that God was to use his Greek text for the basis of the English Bible that was

QUESTION #57

translated with the common man in mind, the King James Bible.

It has been said that "Erasmus laid the egg that Luther hatched." There is probably far more truth to this statement than can be casually discerned. For the reformers were armed with Erasmus's Bible, his writings and his attitude of resistance to Roman Catholic intimidation. Of Luther he said, "I favor Luther as much as I can, even if my cause is everywhere linked with his." He wrote several letters on Luther's behalf, and wholeheartedly agreed with him that salvation was entirely by grace, not works.

He refused pressure by his Roman Catholic superiors to denounce Luther as a heretic. If Erasmus had turned the power of his pen on Luther, it would undoubtedly have caused far more damage than the powerless threats of the pope and his imps were able to do. As it is, only his disagreement with Luther's doctrine of predestination ever prompted him to criticize the Reformer with pen and ink.

Erasmus's greatest point of dissension with the Roman Church was over its doctrine of salvation through works and the tenets of the church.

He taught that salvation was a personal matter between the individual and God and was by faith alone. Of the Roman system of salvation he complained, "Aristotle is so in vogue that there is scarcely time in the churches to interpret the gospel." And what was "the gospel" to which Erasmus referred? We will let him speak for himself.

"Our hope is in the mercy of God and the merits of Christ." Of Jesus Christ he stated, "He...nailed our sins to the cross, sealed our redemption with his blood." He boldly stated that no rites of the Church were necessary for an individual's salvation. "The way to enter Paradise," he said, "is the way of the penitent thief, say simply, Thy will be done. The world to me is crucified and I to the world."

Concerning the most biblical sect of his time, the Anabaptists, he reserved a great deal of respect. He mentioned them as early as 1523 even though he himself was often called the "only Anabaptist of the 16th century." He stated that the Anabaptists that he was familiar with called themselves

152

"Baptists." (Ironically, Erasmus was also the **FIRST** person to use the term "fundamental.")

So we see that when Erasmus died on July 11, 1536, he had led a life that could hardly be construed to be an example of what could be considered a "good Catholic."

But perhaps the greatest compliment, though veiled, that Erasmus's independent nature ever received came in 1559, twenty-three years after his death. That is when Pope Paul IV put Erasmus's writings on the "Index" of books, forbidden to be read by Roman Catholics.

Question #58

QUESTION: How many mistakes are there in the King James Bible?

ANSWER: None.

EXPLANATION: None.

Question #59

QUESTION: I want to be successful in my circle of friends. A stand for the King James Bible would be a detriment to my future promotion. What should I do?

ANSWER: Either stand for God's Bible and trust **HIM** to promote you, or sell out your integrity and grovel for your peers as a dog does for a bone. The choice is yours.

Question #60

QUESTION: What about a contradiction that can't be successfully explained?

ANSWER: You will have to accept the perfection of the Authorized Version by faith.

EXPLANATION: Many years ago the phone in my kitchen rang. On the line was a young man who was a student in a class I was teaching in a nearby Bible College.

He said that his pastor had showed him a contradiction in the King James Bible. (Great "man of faith.") He asked if I could explain it. As he began to tell me the contradiction, I, being familiar with the argument, finished quoting it.

"Oh, you know about it then?" he asked.

"Sure," I replied.

"What's the answer?" he urged expectantly.

"I don't know," I answered, knowing what I had just done to his faith in me. (In **me**, that is.)

I explained my reply to him as I will now explain it to you.

NO ONE can have **ALL** of the answers. There are two reasons for this.

First, if I or any other defender of the Authorized Version had **ALL** of the answers, we would be GOD. But there are innumerable differences between our infinite GOD and His finite creatures. Thus, although some can have many answers, and a few can have a great many answers, **no one** can have **ALL** of the answers.

Second, and most importantly, if we could get ALL of our

questions answered then concerning the Bible issue, we would be walking by **sight** not by **faith**. (Hebrews 11:6, II Corinthians 5:7)

I believe there will **always** have to be **some** questions which remain unexplainable by our human reason. This would make our **FINAL** judgment on the infallibility of the Bible contingent on the reliability of God's statements such as Psalm 12:6,7 and Matthew 24:35 instead of the education and intellect of our favorite "defenders of the faith."

Of course, the proponent of the Authorized Version feels a little vulnerable with this conclusion. Knowing that our antagonists will be quick to exploit what they perceive as a hole in our armor. **BUT** a resort to "faith" as our final and "last ditch" defense is **not** as inconsistent or precarious as it first might seem.

Not inconsistent, because, as previously stated, God would rather we have faith in Him in the face of the unexplainable, as so many of the Old and New Testament saints have exhibited, than to have faith in our own **human** ability to "find an answer" concerning difficult passages.

It is certainly not precarious in that it **does not** leave us at the mercy of our vindictive opponents. For believing in the perfection of a Book which **we can hold in our hands** is surely not as vulnerable as a **professed faith** in the perfection of some **lost originals**.

The reason most critics are so vehement about the infallibility of the originals is because they know that the originals can NEVER be produced, so their **faith** can never be tried or upended.

We are willing, on the other hand, to take the abuse from our "self conceited brethren" and give answers for our reasonable faith in a **tangible** Book rather than in an **idealistic** original. We need not apologize.

Question #61

QUESTION: What if there really ARE mistakes in the King James Bible?

ANSWER: Then it's up to YOU to find the Book that God was talking about in Psalm 12:6,7 and Jesus was talking about in Matthew 24:35.

EXPLANATION: I learned a great lesson in the late 1960's. I watched on television as riotous hippies burned down the Bank of America offices. Other rioters razed entire neighborhoods to the chant of "Burn, Baby, Burn." The hippies' claim was that they had to burn this country to the ground in order to build a new one. And **THAT** is what I learned: ANY hippie can **burn down** a building, but I've **NEVER** seen even **one** building that a hippie built.

The cruel truth is that when you become a rebel against authority, such as the hippies were, you become an EXPERT in the art of destruction (II Peter 2:9-15). A life committed to destroying is difficult to reverse. Thus, hippies know how to **destroy** buildings **which were built by others**. But they cannot **build** anything in a **productive** manner that **improves** on what they destroyed.

This rebellious hatred for AUTHORITY is also manifested in the rabid attacks on the Holy Bible by self-proclaimed scholars. They can wax eloquent in their destructive criticism of God's perfect Book. Then after reducing it to ashes in the hearts and minds of students and church members, are **unable** to replace it with anything that even compares with the divine writings they have so viciously attacked.

If you have been convinced by some spiritual hippie that the King James Bible has mistakes in it, then I suggest you ask them to **REPLACE** it with a Bible that is **perfect**.

They may point to the New International Version, or New American Standard Version, or New King James Version as a "better translation." But none will **DARE** to claim that any of these are the Bible referred to in Psalm 12:6,7 or Matthew 24:35.

If you **press** the issue they will most likely run you through the brambles and briers of the claim that God's Word is found only in "the Greek." But the **fact** is that their very limited knowledge of the original languages leaves them unable to read, study or preach from either Hebrew or Greek. Even if they COULD translate either the Textus Receptus or the local Egyptian text of Alexandria literally, they would be forced to admit that there are readings in both that they cannot accept as infallible.

The **FACT** is, that, like their hippie counterparts of the late 1960's they find themselves standing on a pile of smoldering ruins, without any ability whatsoever to rebuild even an outhouse, let alone render a perfect Bible.

No, if you have been convinced by someone that the King James Bible has errors **IN SPITE** of the facts, then you have accepted that thesis for only one reason; your love for and loyalty to the Bible's antagonist. The critic is your father, brother, pastor, youth director, college professor, or just someone you love too much to confront or withstand on the Bible issue.

So, if you have been convinced by someone that the Authorized Version has mistakes in it, you should toss your King James Bible into the wastebasket **on top of** your NIV, NASV, NKJV and both of the Greek texts. Then go to that person, fall on your knees, kiss their ring and say, "Lord, what wilt thou have me to do?"

But remember one thing: Your God is a **REBELLIOUS HIPPIE!**

Question #62

QUESTION: I'm convinced that the King James Bible is the infallible Word of God. Now what should I do?

ANSWER: Act like you believe it.

EXPLANATION: If you REALLY believe that the Bible (AV 1611) is the infallible, perfect word of God, you will first begin to READ IT. There is no excuse for any Christian to **NOT** be reading the Bible through from cover to cover. Why do you think He gave it to you?

Put away all of the other versions, all your commentaries, all of your ''study helps'' and simply read God's Book. **Remember** the **Author** resides within you (I Corinthians 6:19,20) so He **should** be able to help you to understand it.

Start your reading with the Gospel of John and read to the end of the New Testament. Read at least ten pages a day. **That's not too much to ask**! God has gone to **a lot** of trouble to put that Book in your hand. You can go to a **little** trouble to put it in your heart. After finishing Revelation, go to Genesis and read to John. **THAT'S ONCE**! Now start again! Read it every day that you are alive until the Lord comes back.

Beware! There will be days that you read and don't feel like you ''got'' anything. There **will** be days when the reading seems ''dry'' such as the first nine chapters of I Chronicles. There **will** be days when you are extremely busy. There **will** be whole passages that you don't understand. **NONE** of these circumstances are valid reasons to quit reading. If you can continue to read ten pages a day under the conditions mentioned above, you will have passed one of the greatest tests of character known to man.

Remember. Besides the dry days, you **will** have days when that Book gently settles your heart and mind. You **will** have days when you will learn new truths. And perhaps most importantly, you will get to **know** your God and Saviour in a most personal way.

Secondly, you don't need to go on a rampage against your preacher, teachers or friends who don't believe it. Having read this book you should be equipped to answer most of their protests with grace. You may want to secure another copy to pass along to them. But REMEMBER - this is a **HEART** matter, not a **head** matter. Their final acceptance will rely on whether they, or you for that matter, can find it within themselves to **humble** themselves and accept God's Book as perfect. It will be a high pressure decision, but will depend on which they choose to be more loyal to. Their Saviour and God,or their friends and school.

If you are a preacher, you will have to remove those little so called ''nuggets'' from the imperfect Greek. You will find that building your people's confidence in God's perfect Bible and encouraging them to read it will be much more gratifying for both you and them. Remember, a congregation that is ''in their Bibles'' and reading it, is no threat to a pastor who is ''in **his** Bible'' and reading it.

If you have a friend, a professor or pastor who changes the Bible whom you love and respect dearly, **continue** to love and respect them. But when they ''correct'' or attack God's Book simply discount it from their message. Some may reject you. Some may put pressure on you. Remember. To have to admit that they have been ''wrong all those years'' is extremely difficult for the heart to accept. If they finally reject the Book they will also finally reject you.Continue to love them, but don't let your love/respect allow you to compromise God's Truth. Don't forget that we owe **Him** far more than any man. Now, get busy reading your perfect Bible!

Appendix #1

JOHN 21:15-17 - AGAPE vs PHILEO

I - Comparison: How **Jesus** used AGAPE and PHILEO.

A	1.	Luke 11:42	*the love of God*
A	2.	John 5:42	*the love of God*
P	3.	Matt 10:37	*He that loveth father or mother*
A	4.	Rev 3:9	*to know that I have loved*
P	5.	Rev 3:19	*As many as I love*
P	6.	Matt 23:6	*love the uppermost rooms*
P	7.	John 12:25	*He that loveth his life*
A	8.	Luke 11:43	*ye love the uppermost seats*
P	9.	John 5:20	*the Father loveth the Son*
P	10.	John 16:27	*the Father Himself loveth you, because ye have loved me*

II - Comparison: How **other New Testament writers** used AGAPE and PHILEO.

P	1.	II Tim 3:4	*of pleasures more than of God*
A	2.	John 11:5	*Jesus loved Martha*
P	3.	John 20:2	*the other disciples whom Jesus loved*
P	4.	I Cor 16:22	*If any man love not the Lord*
A	5.	Rom 5:8	*But God commendeth his love*
A	6.	I Cor 16:24	*My love be with you all*
A	7.	II Tim 1:7	*of power, and of love, and...*

P	8.	Rom 12:10	*one to another with brotherly love*
A	9.	II Thes 3:12	*abound in love one toward another*
P	10.	Titus 2:4	*women to be sober, to love their husbands*
A	11.	Eph 5:28	*So ought men to love their wives*
A	12.	I Peter 2:17	*Love the brotherhood*
P	13.	Heb 13:1	*Let brotherly love continue*
P	14.	Titus 3:4	*and love of God our Saviour*
A	15.	I John 2:5	*in him verily is the love of God perfected*

Appendix #2

GLOSSARY OF TEXT NAMES

ANTIOCH

Antiochian Text
Byzantine Text
Syrian Text
Majority Text
Universal Text
Reformation Text
Imperial Text
Traditional Text
Textus Receptus

ALEXANDRIA

Alexandrian Text
Egyptian Text
Local Text
Hesychian Text
Minority Text

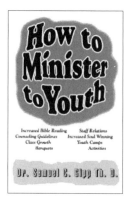

How to Minister to Youth
by Dr. Samuel C. Gipp Th. D.
Dr. Gipp now reveals the secret of his success. If you are a Pastor, Youth Director or Youth Worker you may find the resources in this book invaluable.
ISBN: 1-890120-07-3 $14.95

Living With Pain *A Story of Encouragement*
By Dr. Samuel C. Gipp Th. D.
Samuel Gipp 23 years of age, had recently graduated from Bible College and had entered the field of evangelism. Through an unfortunate accident this was postponed for a year with a broken neck. Misdiagnosed, he went almost three months before it was finally corrected with the broken vertebrae being surgically fused to an undamaged one. With this operation he thought that his ordeal was over. But it was just beginning! Over twenty years have passed and Dr. Gipp is reminded everyday of that hot August day. Reminded by his constant companion-pain.
ISBN 1-890120-02-2 $5.99

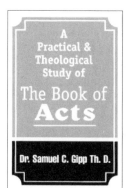

A Practical & Theological Study of the Book of Acts
By Dr. Samuel C. Gipp Th. D.
Dr. Gipp takes a difficult and sometimes misunderstood book of the Bible and lays it out in an easy to understand manner. Great for Bible studies or Sunday School classes.
ISBN. 1-890120-06-5 $14.95